Perfect Vegetarian One Pot Recipes Cookbook

Authentic Dishes Easy Instructions Vibrant Photos

By Grace Morgan

Copyright © by Grace Morgan

No part of this publication may be reproduced, distributed, or transmitted in any form or by any means, including photocopying, recording, or other electronic or mechanical methods, without prior written permission from the author, except for brief quotations used in reviews or other non-commercial purposes permitted by copyright law.

This book is intended to provide readers with a curated collection of vegetarian one-pot recipes. Each recipe has been tested and refined to ensure simplicity, delicious flavors, and ease of preparation, making it suitable for cooks of all skill levels. However, this book is for informational purposes only, and the author and publisher disclaim any liability arising from the use or misuse of the content presented.

Disclaimer: The recipes and techniques shared in this book are based on the author's culinary expertise and personal approach to vegetarian cooking. Readers are encouraged to adapt recipes to meet their individual dietary preferences and consult with a licensed nutritionist or healthcare provider for specific health concerns or requirements.

Amazon KDP Edition

This book has been published through Amazon Kindle Direct Publishing (KDP) and is protected under United States and international copyright laws. Unauthorized reproduction, distribution, or commercial use of this content in any form is strictly prohibited and may result in legal action.

All photographs included in this publication are original works by the author and are intended to guide and inspire readers in recreating these recipes. These images are copyrighted and may not be reproduced or used outside of this book.

Introduction

Welcome to the **Perfect Vegetarian One Pot Recipes Cookbook**, your go-to guide for creating flavorful, wholesome meals in just one pot! Whether you're a seasoned vegetarian or exploring plant-based cooking, this cookbook simplifies your kitchen routine while delivering dishes that delight your taste buds.

Imagine crafting hearty, flavorful meals with minimal cleanup. The **Perfect Vegetarian One Pot Recipes Cookbook** is designed to make cooking effortless and enjoyable, all while enhancing your culinary creativity.

This cookbook features **50 authentic and original recipes**, thoughtfully organized into five chapters to suit every mealtime:

- ✓ **Breakfasts**: Start your day with nourishing, one-pot wonders that energize and satisfy.
- ✓ **Lunch**: Discover hearty midday meals perfect for workdays or leisurely afternoons.
- ✓ **Dinners**: Indulge in comforting, wholesome dishes that bring family and friends together.
- ✓ **Salads**: Elevate your greens with unique, flavor-packed one-pot creations.
- ✓ **Soup**: Cozy up with rich, satisfying soups perfect for any season.

Each recipe has been carefully tested to ensure **perfect flavors and textures** while keeping preparation simple.

Here's why the **Perfect Vegetarian One Pot Recipes Cookbook** is a must-have:

- ✓ **50 Authentic Recipes**: Crafted to highlight the best of vegetarian cooking.
- ✓ **Original, Colorful Photos**: Inspiring visuals accompany every recipe.
- ✓ **Easy-to-Follow Instructions**: Perfect for cooks of all skill levels.
- ✓ **Standard Color Printing for Paperback**: A visually stunning and practical addition to your kitchen.
- ✓ **Flawless Content**: Professionally edited for error-free reading and cooking.

Dive into the **Perfect Vegetarian One Pot Recipes Cookbook** and make plant-based cooking a breeze. From breakfast to dinner, these recipes offer endless variety and convenience. Let's get cooking and create meals that are as delightful to make as they are to eat!

Table of Contents

Chapter 01: Morning Delights

Recipe 01: Vegan Mushroom Pasta Sauce

Experience the rich flavors of this vegan mushroom pasta sauce, a delightful addition to any vegetarian breakfast table. Crafted in one pot, it offers a hearty start to your day with minimal cleanup.

Servings: 4

Cook Time: 20 minutes

Prepping Time: 10 minutes

Difficulty: Easy

Ingredients:

- ✓ 1 tbsp olive oil
- ✓ 4 cloves garlic, minced
- ✓ 1 onion, finely chopped
- ✓ 2 cups sliced mushrooms
- ✓ 1 can (14 oz) diced tomatoes
- ✓ 1 tsp dried basil
- ✓ 1 tsp dried oregano
- ✓ Salt and pepper, to taste
- ✓ 1/4 cup nutritional yeast (for a cheesy flavor)

Step-by-Step Preparation:

1. Heat the olive oil in a large skillet over medium heat.
2. Add garlic and onion, sautéing until translucent.
3. Stir in mushrooms and cook until they begin to soften.
4. Pour the diced tomatoes and add basil, oregano, salt, and pepper.
5. Simmer for 15 minutes, allowing flavors to meld together.
6. Sprinkle in nutritional yeast and stir well until combined.
7. Cook for an additional 5 minutes, then remove from heat.

Nutritional Facts: (Per serving)

- ❖ Calories: 98
- ❖ Protein: 4g
- ❖ Fat: 4g
- ❖ Carbohydrates: 13g
- ❖ Fiber: 3g
- ❖ Sugar: 5g

Savor the simplicity and earthy goodness of this vegan mushroom pasta sauce. Perfect for a cozy breakfast, it pairs beautifully with your favorite pasta or as a rich sauce over toasted bread. Enjoy the ease and taste of a gourmet breakfast at home!

Recipe 02: Balsamic Roasted Vegetables

Start your morning with a burst of color and flavor! These balsamic roasted vegetables blend sweet and earthy roots like carrots, sweet potatoes, pumpkin, beetroots, and potatoes with a tangy balsamic glaze, making a vibrant vegetarian breakfast dish.

Servings: 4

Prepping Time: 15 minutes

Cook Time: 40 minutes

Difficulty: Easy

Ingredients:

- ✓ 2 medium carrots, peeled and sliced
- ✓ 1 large sweet potato, peeled and cubed
- ✓ 1 cup pumpkin, peeled and cubed
- ✓ 2 medium beetroots, peeled and cubed
- ✓ 2 large potatoes, peeled and cubed
- ✓ 3 tbsp olive oil
- ✓ 4 tbsp balsamic vinegar
- ✓ 1 tsp salt
- ✓ 1/2 tsp black pepper
- ✓ 1 tsp dried rosemary

Step-by-Step Preparation:

1. Preheat your oven to 400°F (200°C).
2. Combine all the vegetables in a large mixing bowl.
3. Drizzle with olive oil and balsamic vinegar, then sprinkle with salt, pepper, and rosemary. Toss to coat evenly.
4. Spread the vegetables in a single layer on a baking sheet.
5. Roast in the oven for 40 minutes, stirring halfway through, until vegetables are tender and caramelized.

Nutritional Facts: (Per serving)

- ❖ Calories: 220
- ❖ Protein: 4g
- ❖ Fat: 10g
- ❖ Carbohydrates: 31g
- ❖ Fiber: 6g
- ❖ Sugar: 9g

Enjoy these beautifully caramelized vegetables with their rich balsamic glaze. This dish not only fills the kitchen with a delightful aroma but also packs a nutritious punch to energize your day. Perfect for a leisurely weekend breakfast or a colorful brunch!

Recipe 03: Pan Haggerty

Enjoy a hearty start to your day with Pan Haggerty, a classic British dish that combines the comforting flavors of potatoes, onions, and cheese in a delicious one-pot meal. This vegetarian breakfast is filling and easy to make, perfect for busy mornings.

Servings: 4

Prepping Time: 10 minutes

Cook Time: 25 minutes

Difficulty: Easy

Ingredients:

- ✓ 3 large potatoes, thinly sliced
- ✓ 1 large onion, sliced
- ✓ 1 cup shredded Cheddar cheese
- ✓ 2 tablespoons unsalted butter
- ✓ Salt and pepper to taste
- ✓ 1/4 teaspoon smoked paprika (optional)

Step-by-Step Preparation:

1. Melt butter in a large skillet over medium heat and sauté the onions until translucent.

2. Layer half of the potatoes in the skillet, top with half of the sautéed onions and half of the cheese, and season with salt, pepper, and paprika.

3. Repeat the layers with the remaining potatoes, onions, and cheese. Cover and cook over low heat for about 20 minutes, or until the potatoes are tender.

4. Increase the heat to medium-high and cook for another 5 minutes, or until the bottom layer of potatoes is golden and crispy.

5. Invert onto a plate so the crispy side is up and serve immediately.

Nutritional Facts: (Per serving)

- ❖ Calories: 290
- ❖ Protein: 9g
- ❖ Carbohydrates: 38g
- ❖ Fat: 12g
- ❖ Sodium: 220mg
- ❖ Fiber: 5g

Pan Haggerty not only brings warmth and comfort to your breakfast table but also offers the simplicity and efficiency of a one-pot meal. With its cheesy, crispy goodness, this dish will surely become a favorite in your breakfast repertoire.

Recipe 04: Creamy Turmeric & Broccoli Pasta

Start your morning with a burst of flavor from this Creamy Turmeric and Broccoli Pasta, featuring diced tomatoes for a vibrant touch. This vegetarian breakfast dish is not only delicious but also brings a wholesome twist to your first meal of the day.

Servings: 4

Prepping Time: 15 minutes

Cook Time: 20 minutes

Difficulty: Easy

Ingredients:

- 8 oz pasta (preferably whole wheat)
- 1 head of broccoli, cut into florets
- 1 cup diced tomatoes
- 1 onion, finely chopped
- 2 cloves garlic, minced
- 1 teaspoon turmeric powder
- 1 cup heavy cream
- 1 tablespoon olive oil
- Salt and pepper to taste
- Parmesan cheese, grated (for garnish)

Step-by-Step Preparation:

1. Cook pasta according to package instructions until al dente; drain and set aside.
2. In the same pot, heat olive oil over medium heat. Add onions and garlic, cooking until soft and fragrant.
3. Stir in the turmeric powder, then add broccoli and diced tomatoes. Cook for about 5 minutes, until the broccoli is just tender.
4. Lower the heat and pour in the heavy cream, stirring to combine. Allow the sauce to simmer gently for another 5 minutes.
5. Toss the cooked pasta back into the pot with the creamy sauce, mixing well to ensure the pasta is thoroughly coated. Season with salt and pepper.
6. Serve hot, garnished with grated Parmesan cheese.

Nutritional Facts: (Per serving)

- Calories: 380
- Protein: 10g
- Carbohydrates: 45g
- Fat: 18g
- Sodium: 210mg
- Fiber: 4g

This Creamy Turmeric and Broccoli Pasta not only fills your morning with deliciousness but also infuses it with the health benefits of turmeric and broccoli. It's a satisfying way to wake up and energize for the day ahead.

Recipe 05: Spring Pasta With Vegetables

Dive into a light and refreshing start to your day with this One Pot Spring Pasta with Vegetables. Packed with seasonal veggies, this dish is a colorful, nutritious way to kick off your morning with minimal cleanup and maximum flavor.

Servings: 4

Cook Time: 15 minutes

Prepping Time: 10 minutes

Difficulty: Easy

Ingredients:

- ✓ 8 oz spaghetti or angel hair pasta
- ✓ 1 cup asparagus, chopped
- ✓ 1 cup sugar snap peas, trimmed
- ✓ 1 small zucchini, sliced
- ✓ 1/2 cup cherry tomatoes, halved
- ✓ 1 lemon, zested and juiced
- ✓ 2 tablespoons olive oil
- ✓ 1 garlic clove, minced
- ✓ Salt and pepper to taste
- ✓ Fresh basil, chopped (for garnish)
- ✓ Parmesan cheese, shredded (optional for garnish)

Step-by-Step Preparation:

1. In a large pot, bring water to a boil and cook the pasta al dente according to package instructions.
2. During the last 4 minutes of cooking, add asparagus, sugar snap peas, and zucchini to the pot.
3. Drain the pasta and vegetables, returning them to the pot.
4. Stir in olive oil, garlic, lemon zest, and lemon juice. Mix until the pasta and vegetables are well coated.
5. Season with salt and pepper, then toss in the cherry tomatoes.
6. Serve warm, garnished with fresh basil and optional Parmesan cheese.

Nutritional Facts: (Per serving)

- ❖ Calories: 320
- ❖ Protein: 10g
- ❖ Carbohydrates: 49g
- ❖ Fat: 9g
- ❖ Sodium: 30mg
- ❖ Fiber: 5g

This One Pot Spring Pasta with Vegetables is the perfect recipe to bring a touch of spring to your breakfast table. It's quick, colorful, and brimming with freshness, ideal for a busy morning or a leisurely weekend brunch.

Recipe 06: Mushroom Pasta With Vegetables

Begin your morning with a nourishing bowl of Simple One Pot Lighter Healthier Creamy Mushroom Pasta. This dish brings together the earthy flavors of mushrooms and the freshness of garden vegetables, wrapped in a light creamy sauce that is as satisfying as it is healthy.

Servings: 4

Prepping Time: 15 minutes

Cook Time: 20 minutes

Difficulty: Easy

Ingredients:

- ✓ 8 oz whole wheat penne pasta
- ✓ 2 cups sliced mushrooms
- ✓ 1 cup broccoli florets
- ✓ 1 carrot, sliced
- ✓ 1 small onion, diced
- ✓ 2 cloves garlic, minced
- ✓ 1 cup low-fat milk
- ✓ 1 tablespoon olive oil
- ✓ 1 tablespoon whole wheat flour
- ✓ Salt and pepper to taste
- ✓ Fresh parsley, chopped (for garnish)

Step-by-Step Preparation:

1. Heat olive oil in a large pot over medium heat. Add onion and garlic, sautéing until translucent.
2. Add mushrooms and carrots, and cook for about 5 minutes until they begin to soften.
3. Sprinkle flour over the vegetables and stir to coat. Gradually pour in milk while stirring to create a smooth sauce.
4. Add the pasta and enough water to just cover everything. Bring to a boil, then reduce heat and simmer for 10 minutes.
5. Stir in broccoli and continue to cook until the pasta is tender and the sauce has thickened about 5 more minutes.
6. Season with salt and pepper, and garnish with fresh parsley before serving.

Nutritional Facts: (Per serving)

- ❖ Calories: 295
- ❖ Protein: 12g
- ❖ Carbohydrates: 52g
- ❖ Fat: 6g
- ❖ Sodium: 70mg
- ❖ Fiber: 8g

This Creamy Mushroom Pasta is a wonderful way to start your day with a touch of indulgence without the guilt. It's a hearty, flavorful breakfast option that will leave you satisfied and ready to tackle your day.

Recipe 07: One Pot Zucchini Pasta

Whip up a delightful One Pot of Zucchini Pasta topped with cheese for a quick, nutritious start to your day. This vegetarian breakfast is loaded with the fresh taste of zucchini and the comforting warmth of melted cheese, all brought together in one easy pot.

Servings: 4

Prepping Time: 10 minutes

Cook Time: 15 minutes

Difficulty: Easy

Ingredients:

- ✓ 8 oz linguine or spaghetti
- ✓ 2 medium zucchinis, thinly sliced
- ✓ 1 cup grated mozzarella cheese
- ✓ 2 cloves garlic, minced
- ✓ 2 tablespoons olive oil
- ✓ Salt and pepper to taste
- ✓ Fresh basil leaves, for garnish

Step-by-Step Preparation:

1. In a large pot, heat olive oil over medium heat and sauté garlic until fragrant, about 1 minute.
2. Add the sliced zucchini and cook for 3-4 minutes until slightly tender.
3. Pour in enough water to slightly cover the zucchini and bring to a boil.
4. Add the pasta to the pot, cooking according to package instructions until al dente; stir occasionally to prevent sticking.
5. Once the pasta is cooked, remove from heat and stir in the grated mozzarella cheese until melted and evenly distributed.
6. Season with salt and pepper, and garnish with fresh basil before serving.

Nutritional Facts: (Per serving)

- ❖ Calories: 320
- ❖ Protein: 14g
- ❖ Carbohydrates: 45g
- ❖ Fat: 10g
- ❖ Sodium: 180mg
- ❖ Fiber: 3g

Enjoy this simple, cheesy One Pot Zucchini Pasta as a bright and satisfying way to start your morning. It combines the ease of a one-pot meal with the comfort of home-cooked pasta, perfect for those busy mornings or when you crave a lighter start to the day.

Recipe 08: Vegetarian Potato Paprikash

Savor the rich flavors of Hungarian cuisine right from your breakfast table with this Vegetarian Potato Paprikash. This simple, comforting dish features potatoes seasoned with sweet paprika for a smoky, satisfying start to the day, all from one pot.

Servings: 4

Cook Time: 25 minutes

Prepping Time: 10 minutes

Difficulty: Easy

Ingredients:

- ✓ 4 large potatoes, peeled and diced
- ✓ 1 large onion, chopped
- ✓ 2 cloves garlic, minced
- ✓ 2 tablespoons sweet paprika
- ✓ 1 teaspoon smoked paprika (optional for a smoky flavor)
- ✓ 1 cup vegetable broth
- ✓ 1/2 cup sour cream (use plant-based for the vegan version)
- ✓ 2 tablespoons olive oil
- ✓ Salt and pepper to taste
- ✓ Fresh parsley, chopped (for garnish)

Step-by-Step Preparation:

1. Heat olive oil in a large pot over medium heat. Add the onion and garlic, sautéing until they are soft and translucent.
2. Stir in the sweet and smoked paprika, coating the onions and garlic evenly.
3. Add the diced potatoes and toss to coat them with the paprika mixture.
4. Pour in the vegetable broth, bring to a boil, then reduce heat to a simmer. Cover and cook for about 20 minutes, or until the potatoes are tender.
5. Stir in the sour cream and cook for an additional 5 minutes, until the sauce is creamy and heated through.
6. Season with salt and pepper to taste.
7. Serve hot, garnished with chopped parsley.

Nutritional Facts: (Per serving)

- ❖ Calories: 280
- ❖ Protein: 5g
- ❖ Carbohydrates: 45g
- ❖ Fat: 8g
- ❖ Sodium: 250mg
- ❖ Fiber: 6g

This Vegetarian Potato Paprikash is not only a hearty, cozy breakfast choice but also a vibrant dish to wake up to, offering a perfect blend of spices and textures that will keep you satisfied throughout the morning.

Recipe 09: Whole Wheat Spaghetti

Kick off your morning with a plate of Healthy Whole Wheat Spaghetti, a savory blend of sautéed mushrooms, garlic, and zucchini, all topped with a sprinkle of grated cheese and fresh basil. This vegetarian one-pot breakfast combines nutritious ingredients and delicious flavors for a satisfying start to any day.

Servings: 4

Prepping Time: 10 minutes

Cook Time: 20 minutes

Difficulty: Easy

Ingredients:

- ✓ 8 oz whole wheat spaghetti
- ✓ 2 cups mushrooms, sliced
- ✓ 1 zucchini, sliced
- ✓ 2 cloves garlic, minced
- ✓ 1/4 cup grated Parmesan cheese
- ✓ 1/4 cup fresh basil leaves, chopped
- ✓ 2 tablespoons olive oil
- ✓ Salt and pepper to taste

Step-by-Step Preparation:

1. Cook whole wheat spaghetti in a large pot of boiling salted water according to package directions until al dente; drain and set aside.
2. In the same pot, heat olive oil over medium heat. Add garlic and sauté for about 1 minute until fragrant.
3. Add mushrooms and zucchini to the pot, cooking until vegetables are tender and golden, about 8-10 minutes.
4. Toss the cooked spaghetti back into the pot with the sautéed vegetables. Mix well to combine.
5. Season with salt and pepper, then sprinkle with grated Parmesan cheese.
6. Serve hot, garnished with chopped basil leaves.

Nutritional Facts: (Per serving)

- ❖ Calories: 290
- ❖ Protein: 12g
- ❖ Carbohydrates: 49g
- ❖ Fat: 7g
- ❖ Sodium: 150mg
- ❖ Fiber: 7g

This Healthy Whole Wheat Spaghetti offers a flavorful, wholesome meal to power through your morning, blending the robust tastes of sautéed mushrooms and zucchini with the subtle kick of garlic, all crowned with cheese and basil for a fresh, culinary delight.

Recipe 10: Pasta With Vegetables and Basil

Embrace the fresh, vibrant flavors of Vegan Pasta with Vegetables and Basil, a perfect one-pot breakfast to start your day healthily and deliciously. This dish is packed with a variety of vegetables and infused with the aromatic touch of fresh basil, offering a fulfilling and nutritious meal.

Servings: 4

Prepping Time: 15 minutes

Cook Time: 15 minutes

Difficulty: Easy

Ingredients:

- ✓ 8 oz whole wheat penne pasta
- ✓ 1 cup cherry tomatoes, halved
- ✓ 1 zucchini, diced
- ✓ 1 bell pepper, diced
- ✓ 1 cup spinach leaves
- ✓ 1/4 cup fresh basil, chopped
- ✓ 3 cloves garlic, minced
- ✓ 2 tablespoons olive oil
- ✓ Salt and pepper to taste

Step-by-Step Preparation:

1. Cook pasta in a large pot of boiling salted water according to package instructions until al dente; drain and set aside.
2. In the same pot, heat olive oil over medium heat. Add garlic and sauté until fragrant, about 1 minute.
3. Add bell pepper and zucchini to the pot and cook until they start to soften about 5 minutes.
4. Stir in cherry tomatoes and spinach, cooking until the spinach is wilted, about 2 minutes.
5. Toss the cooked pasta back into the pot with the vegetables. Add chopped basil, salt, and pepper, mixing well to combine.
6. Heat through for an additional 2 minutes to allow flavors to meld.

Nutritional Facts: (Per serving)

- ❖ Calories: 280
- ❖ Protein: 9g
- ❖ Carbohydrates: 47g
- ❖ Fat: 7g
- ❖ Sodium: 30mg
- ❖ Fiber: 8g

This Vegan Pasta with Vegetables and Basil is not only a delight to the senses but also a powerhouse of nutrients, making it an ideal way to fuel your morning with energy and taste.

Chapter 02: Midday Feasts

Recipe 11: One Pot Chickpea Lentil Dish

Delve into the rich and nourishing flavors of Bottle Gourd Curry with Lentils, a one-pot meal that combines chickpeas, lentils, and a medley of vegetables simmered with aromatic spices. This vegetarian lunch is not only easy to prepare but also provides a satisfying, wholesome meal that's perfect for any day of the week.

Servings: 4

Prepping Time: 15 minutes

Cook Time: 30 minutes

Difficulty: Medium

Ingredients:

- ✓ 1 medium bottle gourd, peeled and diced
- ✓ 1 cup lentils, rinsed
- ✓ 1 cup chickpeas, cooked or canned
- ✓ 1 large onion, finely chopped
- ✓ 2 tomatoes, chopped
- ✓ 3 cloves garlic, minced
- ✓ 1 inch ginger, grated
- ✓ 2 teaspoons cumin seeds
- ✓ 1 teaspoon turmeric powder
- ✓ 1 teaspoon coriander powder
- ✓ 1/2 teaspoon garam masala
- ✓ 2 tablespoons vegetable oil
- ✓ Salt to taste
- ✓ Fresh cilantro, chopped for garnish
- ✓ 2 cups water

Step-by-Step Preparation:

1. Heat oil in a large pot over medium heat. Add cumin seeds and let them sizzle for a few seconds.
2. Add the onions, garlic, and ginger, sautéing until onions are golden.
3. Stir in the turmeric, coriander, and garam masala, cooking for about a minute until fragrant.
4. Add the bottle gourd, tomatoes, lentils, chickpeas, and water. Bring to a boil, then reduce heat to low, cover, and simmer for 25-30 minutes, or until the lentils are tender and the curry has thickened.
5. Season with salt and garnish with fresh cilantro before serving.

Nutritional Facts: (Per serving)

- ❖ Calories: 295
- ❖ Protein: 18g
- ❖ Carbohydrates: 45g
- ❖ Fat: 7g
- ❖ Sodium: 300mg
- ❖ Fiber: 15g

Enjoy this Bottle Gourd Curry with Lentils as a comforting and hearty lunch that not only satisfies your hunger but also offers a bounty of nutrients. It's a simple way to bring the essence of authentic flavors to your table with minimal effort.

Recipe 12: Palak Khichdi

Experience the wholesome goodness of Palak Khichdi, a one-pot Indian comfort food that combines basmati rice, yellow mung lentils, and spinach into a nourishing meal. This dish is beautifully seasoned with spices to offer a balance of flavors that are both soothing and satisfying.

Servings: 4

Prepping Time: 20 minutes

Cook Time: 30 minutes

Difficulty: Easy

Ingredients:

- ✓ 1 cup basmati rice
- ✓ 1/2 cup yellow mung lentils
- ✓ 2 cups spinach, blanched and pureed
- ✓ 1 onion, finely chopped
- ✓ 2 cloves garlic, minced
- ✓ 1 teaspoon cumin seeds
- ✓ 1/2 teaspoon turmeric powder
- ✓ 1/2 teaspoon garam masala
- ✓ 2 tablespoons ghee or oil
- ✓ Salt to taste
- ✓ 4 cups water

Step-by-Step Preparation:

1. Rinse the rice and lentils under cold water until the water runs clear.
2. Heat ghee in a large pot over medium heat. Add cumin seeds and let them sputter.
3. Add onions and garlic, sautéing until they turn translucent.
4. Stir in turmeric and garam masala, cooking for a minute until the spices release their aroma.
5. Add the rice, lentils, spinach puree, and water to the pot. Stir well.
6. Bring to a boil, then reduce the heat to low, cover, and simmer for about 20 minutes or until both the rice and lentils are cooked and the mixture has a creamy consistency.
7. Season with salt and adjust the spices as desired.

Nutritional Facts: (Per serving)

- ❖ Calories: 320
- ❖ Protein: 12g
- ❖ Carbohydrates: 58g
- ❖ Fat: 6g
- ❖ Sodium: 70mg
- ❖ Fiber: 6g

Enjoy Palak Khichdi as a fulfilling meal that not only warms your soul but also packs a nutritious punch. It's perfect for anyone looking for a comforting, easy-to-make lunch that's loaded with flavor and health benefits.

Recipe 13: Braised Garden Vegetables

Enjoy a delightful taste of the French countryside with this healthy Vegetable Ratatouille. This vibrant stew of braised garden vegetables embodies the essence of simple, rustic cooking. It's a colorful, nutritious dish that brings the freshness of summer to your lunchtime, no matter the season.

Servings: 4

Prepping Time: 15 minutes

Cook Time: 40 minutes

Difficulty: Easy

Ingredients:

- ✓ 1 eggplant, cubed
- ✓ 2 zucchinis, sliced
- ✓ 1 bell pepper, chopped
- ✓ 1 onion, chopped
- ✓ 3 tomatoes, diced
- ✓ 3 cloves garlic, minced
- ✓ 2 tablespoons olive oil
- ✓ 1 teaspoon dried thyme
- ✓ 1 teaspoon dried basil
- ✓ Salt and pepper to taste
- ✓ Fresh basil for garnish

Step-by-Step Preparation:

1. Heat olive oil in a large pot over medium heat. Add onions and garlic, cooking until soft and translucent.
2. Add eggplant and bell pepper to the pot, cooking for about 5 minutes until they begin to soften.
3. Stir in zucchini and tomatoes, and sprinkle with dried thyme and basil. Season with salt and pepper.
4. Reduce heat to low, cover, and let the vegetables simmer for 30 minutes, stirring occasionally, until all vegetables are tender and the flavors have melded together.
5. Adjust seasoning as needed and garnish with fresh basil before serving.

Nutritional Facts: (Per serving)

- ❖ Calories: 140
- ❖ Protein: 3g
- ❖ Carbohydrates: 20g
- ❖ Fat: 7g
- ❖ Sodium: 20mg
- ❖ Fiber: 6g

This Vegetable Ratatouille is more than just a meal; it's a healthy, heartwarming dish that captures the spirit of mindful cooking and eating. Serve it up for a comforting lunch that satisfies both the palate and the soul.

Recipe 14: Pumpkin Cottage Cheese Rice

Revel in the delightful flavors of autumn with Pumpkin Cottage Cheese Rice. This one-pot dish combines aromatic basmati rice with the sweet, earthy tones of pumpkin, and is enriched with golden, pan-fried cottage cheese cubes. It's a wholesome, comforting meal that's perfect for a cozy lunch.

Servings: 4

Cook Time: 30 minutes

Prepping Time: 20 minutes

Difficulty: Easy

Ingredients:

- 1 cup basmati rice
- 2 cups grated pumpkin
- 1 cup cottage cheese, cut into cubes
- 1 onion, finely chopped
- 2 cloves garlic, minced
- 1 teaspoon cumin seeds
- 1/2 teaspoon turmeric powder
- 1/2 teaspoon garam masala
- 2 tablespoons olive oil
- Salt and pepper to taste
- Fresh cilantro, chopped for garnish

Step-by-Step Preparation:

1. Rinse the basmati rice until the water runs clear, then drain.
2. Heat 1 tablespoon of olive oil in a pot over medium heat. Add cumin seeds and let them sputter. Then add onions and garlic, cooking until they turn translucent.
3. Stir in grated pumpkin, turmeric, and garam masala, sautéing for a few minutes until the pumpkin softens.
4. Add the rice to the pot along with 2 cups of water. Season with salt and bring to a boil. Reduce heat to low, cover, and simmer until the rice is cooked, about 20 minutes.
5. While the rice cooks, heat the remaining olive oil in a pan over medium heat and pan-fry the cottage cheese cubes until golden brown on all sides.
6. Once the rice is done, gently fold in the fried cottage cheese.
7. Garnish with chopped cilantro before serving.

Nutritional Facts: (Per serving)

- Calories: 320
- Protein: 12g
- Carbohydrates: 45g
- Fat: 10g
- Sodium: 200mg
- Fiber: 2g

This Pumpkin Cottage Cheese Rice offers a unique twist on traditional rice dishes, blending the natural sweetness of pumpkin with the creamy texture of cottage cheese for a nourishing lunch that warms the heart and delights the palate.

Recipe 15: Sambar Rice or Sambar Sadam

Discover the heartwarming flavors of Sambar Rice, a beloved one-pot meal hailing from the lush landscapes of Tamil Nadu and Kerala. This comforting South Indian dish combines aromatic rice with lentils and a medley of vegetables, all simmered in a tamarind-infused sambar spice blend, making it a wholesome and satisfying lunch option.

Servings: 4

Prepping Time: 15 minutes

Cook Time: 40 minutes

Difficulty: Medium

Ingredients:

- 1 cup rice
- 1/2 cup toor dal (split pigeon peas)
- 1 carrot, chopped
- 1 small eggplant, chopped
- 1 potato, cubed
- 1 onion, sliced
- 1 tomato, chopped
- 1/4 cup tamarind extract
- 2 tablespoons sambar powder
- 1 teaspoon mustard seeds
- 1 teaspoon cumin seeds
- 2 dry red chilies
- A pinch of asafoetida (hing)
- 3 tablespoons vegetable oil
- Salt to taste
- Fresh coriander, chopped for garnish
- 4 cups water

Step-by-Step Preparation:

1. Rinse the rice and toor dal thoroughly; soak together for 30 minutes.
2. In a large pot, heat oil over medium heat. Add mustard seeds, cumin seeds, dry red chilies, and a pinch of asafoetida. Let them sizzle until the mustard seeds start popping.
3. Add sliced onions and sauté until they turn golden. Then add chopped vegetables and tomato, cooking for a few minutes until slightly soft.
4. Drain the rice and dal mixture, adding it to the pot along with sambar powder and salt. Stir well to combine.
5. Pour in water and tamarind extract, bring the mixture to a boil, then reduce heat to a simmer. Cover and cook for about 30 minutes, or until the rice and dal are soft and the flavors are well blended.
6. Garnish with chopped coriander before serving.

Nutritional Facts: (Per serving)

- Calories: 350
- Protein: 12g
- Carbohydrates: 65g
- Fat: 7g
- Sodium: 300mg
- Fiber: 8g

Sambar Rice offers a delightful taste experience that brings a slice of South Indian culinary tradition to your table. It's a nutritious, vegan-friendly dish that's perfect for anyone seeking a flavorful, hearty meal.

Recipe 16: Beetroot Pulao

Savor the vibrant and nutritious Beetroot Pulao, a delightful one-pot rice dish that marries the earthy sweetness of beetroot with aromatic basmati rice and spices. Paired with crispy air-fried tofu bites and a side of cooling curd, this meal is a colorful, wholesome choice for any lunchtime.

Servings: 4

Cook Time: 30 minutes

Prepping Time: 15 minutes

Difficulty: Easy

Ingredients:

- ✓ 1 cup basmati rice
- ✓ 2 medium beetroots, grated
- ✓ 1 large onion, sliced
- ✓ 2 cloves garlic, minced
- ✓ 1 teaspoon cumin seeds
- ✓ 1/2 teaspoon garam masala
- ✓ 2 tablespoons vegetable oil
- ✓ Salt to taste
- ✓ 1 cup tofu, cubed
- ✓ 1 cup curd for serving
- ✓ Fresh cilantro, chopped for garnish

Step-by-Step Preparation:

1. Rinse the basmati rice until water runs clear, then soak for 30 minutes.
2. Heat oil in a pot over medium heat. Add cumin seeds and let them sizzle.
3. Add garlic and onions, sautéing until they become translucent.
4. Stir in the grated beetroot and cook for 5 minutes, until it starts to soften.
5. Drain the rice and add to the pot, along with garam masala and salt. Mix well.
6. Add 2 cups of water, bring to a boil, then reduce to a simmer, cover, and cook for 20 minutes until the rice is fluffy and water is absorbed.
7. While the rice cooks, air fry the tofu cubes at 400°F for 15 minutes or until crispy.
8. Serve the pulao hot, topped with air-fried tofu bites and a side of curd, garnished with chopped cilantro.

Nutritional Facts: (Per serving)

- ❖ Calories: 320
- ❖ Protein: 12g
- ❖ Carbohydrates: 54g
- ❖ Fat: 7g
- ❖ Sodium: 300mg
- ❖ Fiber: 3g

Enjoy this Beetroot Pulao as a burst of color and flavor on your dining table, offering a nutritious yet delicious twist to your regular meal routine. It's perfect for those seeking a tasty and fulfilling vegetarian lunch.

Recipe 17: Mexican Tomato Rice

Ignite your palate with the bold flavors of Spicy Tomato Rice with Black Beans, Onions, and Corn. This one-pot vegetarian dish is a fiesta of tastes and textures, offering a hearty and vibrant lunch option that's both satisfying and easy to prepare.

Servings: 4

Prepping Time: 10 minutes

Cook Time: 20 minutes

Difficulty: Easy

Ingredients:

- ✓ 1 cup basmati rice
- ✓ 1 can black beans, drained and rinsed
- ✓ 1 cup corn kernels, fresh or frozen
- ✓ 1 large onion, chopped
- ✓ 2 tomatoes, chopped
- ✓ 2 cloves garlic, minced
- ✓ 1 teaspoon chili powder
- ✓ 1/2 teaspoon cumin powder
- ✓ 2 tablespoons olive oil
- ✓ Salt to taste
- ✓ Fresh cilantro, chopped for garnish
- ✓ 1 lime, cut into wedges for serving

Step-by-Step Preparation:

1. Rinse the basmati rice thoroughly and drain.
2. Heat olive oil in a large pot over medium heat. Add chopped onions and minced garlic, and sauté until onions are translucent.
3. Stir in chili and cumin powders, cooking for a minute until fragrant.
4. Add chopped tomatoes, black beans, and corn to the pot. Cook for 5 minutes, stirring occasionally.
5. Add the rice and 2 cups of water, season with salt, and bring to a boil. Reduce heat to low, cover, and simmer for 18-20 minutes, or until rice is cooked and liquid is absorbed.
6. Fluff the rice gently with a fork, then garnish with chopped cilantro. Serve hot with lime wedges on the side.

Nutritional Facts: (Per serving)

- ❖ Calories: 350
- ❖ Protein: 10g
- ❖ Carbohydrates: 65g
- ❖ Fat: 7g
- ❖ Sodium: 200mg
- ❖ Fiber: 8g

This Spicy Tomato Rice with Black Beans, Onions, and Corn brings a vibrant and flavorful twist to your lunch routine, perfect for those looking for a nutritious and delicious meal that's quick and easy to make.

Recipe 18: Soya Chunks Biryani

Indulge in the rich and aromatic Soya Chunks Biryani, where fluffy basmati rice meets nutritious soya chunks, spices, and vegetables in a delightful symphony of flavors. This vegetarian one-pot dish is a healthful twist on the classic biryani, packed with protein and perfect for any meal.

Servings: 4

Prepping Time: 20 minutes

Cook Time: 30 minutes

Difficulty: Medium

Ingredients:

- 1 cup basmati rice
- 1 cup soya chunks, soaked and drained
- 1 large onion, sliced
- 1 carrot, diced
- 1/2 cup green peas
- 2 tomatoes, chopped
- 2 cloves garlic, minced
- 1-inch piece ginger, grated
- 2 green chilies, slit
- 1 teaspoon cumin seeds
- 2 bay leaves
- 1/2 teaspoon turmeric powder
- 1 teaspoon garam masala
- 2 tablespoons vegetable oil
- Salt to taste
- Fresh mint and cilantro, chopped for garnish
- 2.5 cups water

Step-by-Step Preparation:

1. Rinse the basmati rice until the water runs clear, then soak for 30 minutes.
2. Heat oil in a large pot over medium heat. Add cumin seeds and bay leaves, letting them sizzle for a few seconds.
3. Add sliced onions, garlic, ginger, and green chilies, sautéing until onions are golden.
4. Stir in chopped tomatoes, carrots, and green peas, cooking until vegetables are slightly tender.
5. Add turmeric powder and garam masala, mixing well.
6. Incorporate soya chunks and drained rice into the pot, stirring gently to combine all the ingredients.
7. Pour in water and season with salt. Bring to a boil, then reduce heat to low, cover, and simmer for 20 minutes, or until the rice is cooked and water is absorbed.
8. Remove from heat and let it sit covered for 5 minutes. Fluff with a fork and garnish with fresh mint and cilantro before serving.

Nutritional Facts: (Per serving)

- Calories: 330
- Protein: 15g
- Carbohydrates: 55g
- Fat: 7g
- Sodium: 300mg
- Fiber: 6g

This Soya Chunks Biryani offers a delicious and wholesome approach to traditional biryani, making it an ideal meal for those seeking to enjoy classic flavors with a nutritious twist. Perfect for a hearty lunch or a special occasion!

Recipe 19: Savory Orzo in Rosa Sauce

Explore the creamy delight of Savory Orzo in Rosa Sauce, a one-pot wonder that combines the subtle textures of orzo pasta with a rich and tangy tomato-cream sauce. This dish is sprinkled with chopped green onions for an added burst of flavor, making it a quick, delicious, and satisfying vegetarian lunch option.

Servings: 4

Cook Time: 20 minutes

Prepping Time: 10 minutes

Difficulty: Easy

Ingredients:

- 1 cup orzo pasta
- 1 onion, finely chopped
- 2 cloves garlic, minced
- 1 can (14 oz) crushed tomatoes
- 1/4 cup heavy cream
- 2 tablespoons olive oil
- 1/2 cup green onions, chopped
- Salt and pepper to taste
- Grated Parmesan cheese, for garnish

Step-by-Step Preparation:

1. Heat olive oil in a large pot over medium heat. Add the chopped onion and minced garlic, and sauté until the onion is translucent.

2. Stir in the crushed tomatoes and bring to a simmer. Cook for about 5 minutes to let the flavors meld together.

3. Add the orzo to the pot along with enough water to cover it. Season with salt and pepper.

4. Let the orzo cook in the tomato sauce, stirring occasionally, until it is al dente, about 10 minutes.

5. Stir in the heavy cream and continue to cook for an additional 2-3 minutes, until the sauce is creamy and the orzo is fully cooked.

6. Remove from heat and sprinkle with chopped green onions and grated Parmesan cheese before serving.

Nutritional Facts: (Per serving)

- Calories: 280
- Protein: 8g
- Carbohydrates: 38g
- Fat: 11g
- Sodium: 200mg
- Fiber: 2g

This Savory Orzo in Rosa Sauce offers a perfect blend of creamy texture and robust flavors, ideal for a hearty midday meal. Its simplicity and elegance make it a go-to dish for both quick lunches and relaxed weekend dining.

Recipe 20: Green Peas Pulav

Indulge in the simple yet delicious flavors of Green Peas Pulav, a classic Indian dish where fragrant basmati rice meets the sweetness of green peas, all beautifully seasoned with spices and cooked in rich ghee. This one-pot recipe offers both comfort and taste, making it an excellent choice for a nourishing vegetarian lunch.

Servings: 4

Cook Time: 25 minutes

Prepping Time: 15 minutes

Difficulty: Easy

Ingredients:

- 1 cup basmati rice
- 1 cup fresh green peas
- 2 tablespoons ghee
- 1 onion, thinly sliced
- 2 cloves garlic, minced
- 1 teaspoon cumin seeds
- 1 bay leaf
- 4 cloves
- 1 inch cinnamon stick
- 1/2 teaspoon turmeric powder
- Salt to taste
- 2 cups water
- Fresh cilantro, chopped for garnish

Step-by-Step Preparation:

1. Rinse the basmati rice until the water runs clear, then soak it for 30 minutes.
2. Heat ghee in a large pot over medium heat. Add cumin seeds, bay leaf, cloves, and cinnamon sticks; let them sizzle for a few seconds.
3. Add the sliced onion and garlic, sautéing until the onion turns golden brown.
4. Stir in the turmeric powder, then add the green peas, stirring for a minute to coat them in the spices.
5. Drain the rice and add to the pot, stirring gently to mix with the spices and peas.
6. Pour in water and add salt. Increase the heat and bring to a boil, then reduce the heat to low, cover, and simmer for about 15-20 minutes, or until the rice is cooked and all the water has been absorbed.
7. Fluff the rice with a fork, garnish with chopped cilantro, and serve hot.

Nutritional Facts: (Per serving)

- Calories: 260
- Protein: 6g
- Carbohydrates: 45g
- Fat: 7g
- Sodium: 10mg
- Fiber: 4g

Green Peas Pulav is a delightful dish that brings freshness and aroma to your table, making it the perfect accompaniment to any meal or a satisfying standalone lunch that's both hearty and healthy.

Chapter 03: Evening Comforts

Recipe 21: Homemade Coriander Pulao

Experience the aromatic flavors of Homemade Coriander Pulao, a delightful one-pot dinner crafted with basmati rice, a vibrant green chutney, and whole spices, all sautéed in rich ghee. This dish is perfect for those evenings when you crave something comforting yet light and packed with the fresh essence of coriander.

Servings: 4

Cook Time: 30 minutes

Prepping Time: 20 minutes

Difficulty: Easy

Ingredients:

- 1 cup basmati rice
- 1/2 cup green coriander chutney
- 1 onion, thinly sliced
- 2 tablespoons ghee
- 1 teaspoon cumin seeds
- 2 bay leaves
- 1 cinnamon stick
- 3 cloves
- 3 cardamom pods
- Salt to taste
- 2 cups water
- Fresh coriander leaves for garnish

Step-by-Step Preparation:

1. Wash the rice thoroughly until water runs clear, then soak for 30 minutes.
2. Heat ghee in a pot over medium heat. Add cumin seeds, bay leaves, cinnamon sticks, cloves, and cardamom pods. Let them sizzle until fragrant.
3. Add the sliced onion and sauté until golden and soft.
4. Stir in the green coriander chutney, mixing well to combine with the onions and spices.
5. Drain the rice and add to the pot. Stir gently to coat the rice with the chutney and spice mixture.
6. Add water and salt, bring to a boil, then reduce the heat to low, cover, and simmer until the rice is cooked and all the water is absorbed about 20 minutes.
7. Fluff the pulao with a fork and garnish with fresh coriander leaves before serving.

Nutritional Facts: (Per serving)

- Calories: 240
- Protein: 4g
- Carbohydrates: 38g
- Fat: 8g
- Sodium: 75mg
- Fiber: 2g

Homemade Coriander Pulao serves as a perfect centerpiece for a quiet dinner at home, offering a taste of tradition with a modern twist. It's an easy, flavorful way to end your day on a delicious note.

Recipe 22: Vegetable Tagine One Pot Wonder

Dive into the exotic flavors of a Vegetable Tagine, a Moroccan-inspired one-pot wonder that brings together a medley of vegetables, sweet dried fruits, and bold spices in a hearty and aromatic stew. This dish is a perfect vegetarian dinner option that promises a delightful culinary adventure right at your dining table.

Servings: 4

Prepping Time: 20 minutes

Cook Time: 40 minutes

Difficulty: Medium

Ingredients:

- 2 carrots, sliced
- 2 zucchinis, sliced
- 1 bell pepper, chopped
- 1 sweet potato, cubed
- 1 onion, chopped
- 3 cloves garlic, minced
- 1 cup chickpeas, drained and rinsed
- 1/2 cup dried apricots, chopped
- 1/4 cup raisins
- 2 teaspoons ground cumin
- 1 teaspoon ground cinnamon
- 1 teaspoon ground turmeric
- 1/2 teaspoon ground ginger
- 2 tablespoons olive oil
- 3 cups vegetable broth
- Salt and pepper to taste
- Fresh cilantro, chopped for garnish

Step-by-Step Preparation:

1. Heat olive oil in a large pot or tagine over medium heat. Add onions and garlic, and sauté until softened.
2. Add all the spices—cumin, cinnamon, turmeric, and ginger—stirring continuously to release their aromas.
3. Incorporate carrots, zucchini, bell pepper, and sweet potato, coating them well with the spice mixture.
4. Stir in chickpeas, dried apricots, and raisins. Pour in the vegetable broth and season with salt and pepper.
5. Bring to a boil, then reduce the heat, cover, and simmer for about 30 minutes, or until the vegetables are tender.
6. Adjust seasoning to taste and garnish with fresh cilantro before serving.

Nutritional Facts: (Per serving)

- Calories: 280
- Protein: 7g
- Carbohydrates: 53g
- Fat: 7g
- Sodium: 300mg
- Fiber: 9g

This Vegetable Tagine is not just a meal; it's an experience—an opportunity to enjoy a burst of flavors and textures that nourish the body and delight the senses. Perfect for a cozy evening meal that warms the heart and fills the belly.

Recipe 23: Homemade Veggie Fried Rice

Whip up a quick and delicious dinner with Homemade Veggie Fried Rice, featuring a colorful mix of vegetables and fluffy rice stir-fried to perfection. This simple one-pot dish is a great way to use up leftover rice and veggies, ensuring a satisfying meal that's both easy to prepare and packed with flavor.

Servings: 4

Prepping Time: 10 minutes

Cook Time: 15 minutes

Difficulty: Easy

Ingredients:

- ✓ 2 cups cooked rice (preferably day-old)
- ✓ 1 cup mixed vegetables (carrots, peas, corn)
- ✓ 1 bell pepper, finely chopped
- ✓ 1 onion, chopped
- ✓ 2 cloves garlic, minced
- ✓ 2 tablespoons soy sauce
- ✓ 1 tablespoon sesame oil
- ✓ 2 eggs, beaten (optional)
- ✓ Salt and pepper to taste
- ✓ 2 green onions, sliced for garnish
- ✓ 1 tablespoon vegetable oil

Step-by-Step Preparation:

1. Heat vegetable oil in a large skillet or wok over medium-high heat. Add onions and garlic, and sauté until translucent.

2. Add bell pepper and mixed vegetables, cooking until just tender.

3. Push the veggies to the side of the pan, pour in the beaten eggs (if using), and scramble until just set.

4. Add the cooked rice, breaking up any clumps. Stir in soy sauce and sesame oil, mixing well to combine all ingredients evenly.

5. Cook for an additional 5 minutes, stirring occasionally until everything is heated through and slightly crispy.

6. Season with salt and pepper, then garnish with sliced green onions before serving.

Nutritional Facts: (Per serving)

- ❖ Calories: 280
- ❖ Protein: 7g
- ❖ Carbohydrates: 45g
- ❖ Fat: 8g
- ❖ Sodium: 600mg
- ❖ Fiber: 3g

This Homemade Veggie Fried Rice is not just a meal—it's a versatile, flavorful dish that brings comfort and nutrition to your dinner table in minutes. It's perfect for a busy evening when you need something quick yet fulfilling.

Recipe 24: Spicy Vegetable Stew

Unleash the flavors of this hearty Spicy Stew, a robust blend of red kidney beans, bell peppers, tomatoes, and onions, perfectly seasoned and simmered to bring out a rich, savory taste. Paired with a cooling yogurt dip and slices of fresh bread, this dish is a filling and flavorful vegetarian dinner that's sure to satisfy.

Servings: 4

Prepping Time: 15 minutes

Cook Time: 30 minutes

Difficulty: Easy

Ingredients:

- ✓ 1 cup red kidney beans, soaked overnight and drained
- ✓ 1 bell pepper, diced
- ✓ 1 onion, chopped
- ✓ 2 tomatoes, chopped
- ✓ 2 cloves garlic, minced
- ✓ 1 teaspoon cumin powder
- **For the yogurt dip:**
- ✓ 1 cup plain yogurt
- ✓ 1 tablespoon lemon juice

- ✓ 1/2 teaspoon chili powder
- ✓ 1/4 teaspoon smoked paprika
- ✓ 2 tablespoons olive oil
- ✓ Salt and pepper to taste
- ✓ 2 cups vegetable broth
- ✓ Sliced bread for serving

- ✓ 1 clove garlic, minced
- ✓ Salt and pepper to taste

Step-by-Step Preparation:

1. Heat olive oil in a large pot over medium heat. Add onions and garlic, sautéing until translucent.
2. Add bell pepper and cook for 5 minutes, until slightly softened.
3. Stir in tomatoes, cumin, chili powder, and smoked paprika. Cook for another 5 minutes until the tomatoes break down.
4. Add the kidney beans and vegetable broth. Bring to a boil, then reduce to a simmer. Cover and cook for 20 minutes, or until the beans are tender.
5. For the yogurt dip, combine yogurt, lemon juice, minced garlic, salt, and pepper in a small bowl. Mix well and chill until ready to serve.
6. Season the stew with salt and pepper to taste. Serve hot, accompanied by the yogurt dip and slices of bread.

Nutritional Facts: (Per serving)

- ❖ Calories: 250
- ❖ Protein: 12g
- ❖ Carbohydrates: 35g

- ❖ Fat: 7g
- ❖ Sodium: 480mg
- ❖ Fiber: 9g

This Spicy Stew with Yogurt Dip offers a delightful mix of textures and temperatures, combining the warmth of the stew with the coolness of the yogurt. It's a comforting, nourishing meal that makes any dinner special.

Recipe 25: Vegetarian Lentil One Pot With Carrots

Savor the simplicity and warmth of a Vegetarian Lentil One Pot with Carrots, a wholesome and hearty dish that combines the earthiness of lentils with the natural sweetness of carrots. This one-pot wonder is an easy, nutritious meal that's perfect for a comforting dinner on any day of the week.

Servings: 4

Prepping Time: 10 minutes

Cook Time: 30 minutes

Difficulty: Easy

Ingredients:

- ✓ 1 cup dried green lentils, rinsed and drained
- ✓ 3 large carrots, peeled and diced
- ✓ 1 onion, chopped
- ✓ 2 cloves garlic, minced
- ✓ 1 teaspoon dried thyme
- ✓ 4 cups vegetable broth
- ✓ 2 tablespoons olive oil
- ✓ Salt and pepper to taste
- ✓ Fresh parsley, chopped for garnish

Step-by-Step Preparation:

1. Heat olive oil in a large pot over medium heat. Add onions and garlic, and sauté until onions are translucent.

2. Add carrots and thyme, stirring to combine. Cook for about 5 minutes until carrots start to soften.

3. Stir in the lentils and vegetable broth. Bring to a boil, then reduce heat to low and simmer covered for about 25 minutes, or until the lentils are tender.

4. Season with salt and pepper. Serve hot, garnished with fresh parsley.

Nutritional Facts: (Per serving)

- ❖ Calories: 260
- ❖ Protein: 15g
- ❖ Carbohydrates: 38g
- ❖ Fat: 7g
- ❖ Sodium: 300mg
- ❖ Fiber: 16g

This Vegetarian Lentil One Pot with Carrots is not just a meal—it's a hug in a bowl. Its robust flavors and hearty ingredients make it a satisfying dinner that is as nourishing as it is delicious.

Recipe 26: Vegetable Masala Oats Khichadi

Indulge in the comfort and spice of Vegetable Masala Oats Khichadi, a nutritious twist on the classic Indian dish that combines the health benefits of oats with the vibrant flavors of vegetables and spices. This easy-to-make one-pot dinner is perfect for those seeking a wholesome meal that doesn't compromise on taste.

Servings: 4

Cook Time: 20 minutes

Prepping Time: 10 minutes

Difficulty: Easy

Ingredients:

- ✓ 1 cup rolled oats
- ✓ 1 cup mixed vegetables (carrots, peas, and green beans), chopped
- ✓ 1 onion, finely chopped
- ✓ 2 tomatoes, finely chopped
- ✓ 1 green chili, chopped
- ✓ 1 teaspoon cumin seeds
- ✓ 1/2 teaspoon turmeric powder
- ✓ 1 teaspoon garam masala
- ✓ 1/2 teaspoon mustard seeds
- ✓ 2 tablespoons vegetable oil
- ✓ Salt to taste
- ✓ 3 cups water
- ✓ Fresh cilantro, chopped for garnish

Step-by-Step Preparation:

1. Heat oil in a large pot over medium heat. Add mustard seeds and cumin seeds, letting them crackle for a few seconds.
2. Add the chopped onions and green chili, sautéing until the onions become translucent.
3. Stir in the turmeric powder, then add the chopped vegetables and tomatoes, cooking until they start to soften.
4. Add the oats and water to the pot. Stir in garam masala and salt.
5. Bring the mixture to a boil, then reduce the heat and simmer for about 15 minutes, stirring occasionally, until the oats are cooked and the khichadi has a thick consistency.
6. Garnish with fresh cilantro before serving.

Nutritional Facts: (Per serving)

- ❖ Calories: 190
- ❖ Protein: 5g
- ❖ Carbohydrates: 28g
- ❖ Fat: 7g
- ❖ Sodium: 75mg
- ❖ Fiber: 4g

This Vegetable Masala Oats Khichadi is a delightful, savory meal that combines traditional flavors with the nutritious power of oats, making it ideal for a fulfilling dinner that's as good for you as it tastes.

Recipe 27: Vegetables With Mushrooms

Enjoy a simple yet flavorful Vegetables with Mushrooms dish, a one-pot wonder that brings together a variety of fresh vegetables and earthy mushrooms. This light and healthy dinner option is not only easy to prepare but also rich in nutrients, making it a perfect choice for a quick weeknight meal.

Servings: 4

Cook Time: 20 minutes

Prepping Time: 10 minutes

Difficulty: Easy

Ingredients:

- ✓ 1 cup mushrooms, sliced
- ✓ 1 bell pepper, chopped
- ✓ 1 zucchini, chopped
- ✓ 1 carrot, sliced
- ✓ 1 onion, chopped
- ✓ 2 cloves garlic, minced
- ✓ 2 tablespoons olive oil
- ✓ 1 teaspoon dried thyme
- ✓ Salt and pepper to taste
- ✓ Fresh parsley, chopped for garnish

Step-by-Step Preparation:

1. Heat olive oil in a large skillet over medium heat. Add garlic and onions, sautéing until onions are translucent.

2. Add mushrooms, and cook for about 5 minutes until they begin to brown.

3. Stir in bell pepper, zucchini, and carrot, cooking for another 10 minutes until the vegetables are tender.

4. Season with dried thyme, salt, and pepper.

5. Serve hot, garnished with fresh parsley.

Nutritional Facts: (Per serving)

- ❖ Calories: 110
- ❖ Protein: 3g
- ❖ Carbohydrates: 10g
- ❖ Fat: 7g
- ❖ Sodium: 50mg
- ❖ Fiber: 3g

This Vegetables with Mushrooms dish is a splendid way to enjoy a light, nutritious meal that doesn't skimp on flavor. It's perfect for those evenings when you need something satisfying yet straightforward.

Recipe 28: Creamy Mushroom Risotto

Indulge in the rich and creamy texture of Mushroom Risotto Topped with Herbs, a classic Italian dish that is both comforting and elegant. This vegetarian one-pot dinner combines the earthy flavors of mushrooms with creamy Arborio rice, finished with a sprinkle of fresh herbs for a gourmet touch to your evening meal.

Servings: 4

Cook Time: 25 minutes

Prepping Time: 10 minutes

Difficulty: Medium

Ingredients:

- 1 cup Arborio rice
- 2 cups sliced mushrooms
- 1 onion, finely chopped
- 2 cloves garlic, minced
- 4 cups vegetable broth
- 1/2 cup white wine
- 1/4 cup heavy cream
- 2 tablespoons olive oil
- 1/4 cup grated Parmesan cheese
- Salt and pepper to taste
- Fresh herbs (parsley and thyme), chopped for garnish

Step-by-Step Preparation:

1. In a large saucepan, heat olive oil over medium heat. Add onion and garlic, cooking until soft and translucent.
2. Add the mushrooms and cook until they are golden and their liquid has evaporated.
3. Stir in the Arborio rice, cooking for about 1 minute to toast the grains lightly.
4. Pour in the white wine and cook until mostly absorbed.
5. Add the vegetable broth, one cup at a time, stirring continuously until each addition is absorbed before adding the next.
6. Once the rice is al dente and creamy, stir in the heavy cream and grated Parmesan. Season with salt and pepper to taste.
7. Serve hot, garnished with chopped fresh herbs.

Nutritional Facts: (Per serving)

- Calories: 380
- Protein: 10g
- Carbohydrates: 50g
- Fat: 15g
- Sodium: 870mg
- Fiber: 2g

This Creamy Mushroom Risotto is a delightful blend of simple ingredients and complex flavors, making it a perfect dish for a cozy dinner at home. It's sure to impress with its creamy consistency and savory taste, enhanced by the freshness of aromatic herbs.

Recipe 29: Orzo Primavera With Green Veggies

Delight in the fresh flavors of Orzo Primavera with Green Veggies, a vibrant one-pot meal that perfectly showcases the crispness of seasonal green vegetables. This light yet satisfying dish combines tender orzo pasta with a medley of greens, making it an ideal dinner option for those seeking a nutritious and quick vegetarian meal.

Servings: 4

Prepping Time: 10 minutes

Cook Time: 20 minutes

Difficulty: Easy

Ingredients:

- 1 cup orzo pasta
- 1 cup broccoli florets
- 1 cup snap peas, trimmed
- 1 zucchini, diced
- 1 green bell pepper, diced
- 2 cloves garlic, minced
- 2 tablespoons olive oil
- 1/2 cup grated Parmesan cheese
- Salt and pepper to taste
- Fresh basil, chopped for garnish
- Juice of 1 lemon

Step-by-Step Preparation:

1. In a large skillet, heat olive oil over medium heat. Add garlic and sauté until fragrant.
2. Add broccoli, snap peas, zucchini, and bell pepper to the skillet. Cook for about 5 minutes until the vegetables are just tender.
3. Stir in the orzo and add enough water to cover everything. Bring to a simmer, cover, and cook for 10 minutes, or until the orzo is tender.
4. Remove from heat and stir in the Parmesan cheese. Season with salt and pepper.
5. Squeeze lemon juice over the cooked orzo and vegetables, mixing thoroughly.
6. Serve hot, garnished with fresh basil.

Nutritional Facts: (Per serving)

- Calories: 300
- Protein: 12g
- Carbohydrates: 40g
- Fat: 10g
- Sodium: 200mg
- Fiber: 3g

Orzo Primavera with Green Veggies is not just a meal; it's a celebration of freshness and simplicity. This dish brings the best of the garden to your table, offering a burst of flavor and color that can lighten up any evening.

Recipe 30: Taco Casserole

Embrace a fusion of flavors with this vegetarian twist on classic comfort dishes: Taco Casserole, One Pot Mexican Pasta, and Cheesy Burger Casserole. Each dish offers the cozy satisfaction of a casserole with hearty ingredients and zesty spices, all prepared in one pot for ultimate convenience and minimal cleanup.

Servings: 4

Prepping Time: 20 minutes

Cook Time: 30 minutes

Difficulty: Easy

Ingredients:

- ✓ 1 cup plant-based ground meat (for all three dishes)
- ✓ 8 oz pasta (for Mexican Pasta)
- ✓ 1 onion, diced
- ✓ 2 cloves garlic, minced
- ✓ 1 bell pepper, diced
- ✓ 1 can black beans, drained and rinsed (for Taco Casserole)
- ✓ 1 can diced tomatoes
- ✓ 1 tablespoon taco seasoning
- ✓ 1 teaspoon chili powder
- ✓ 1 cup shredded vegan cheese
- ✓ 2 tablespoons olive oil
- ✓ Salt and pepper to taste
- ✓ Fresh cilantro, chopped for garnish

Step-by-Step Preparation:

1. Heat olive oil in a large pot or skillet over medium heat. Add onions and garlic, cooking until translucent.
2. Stir in plant-based ground meat, breaking it apart as it cooks. Add taco seasoning and chili powder.
3. For the Taco Casserole: Add black beans and half of the diced tomatoes to the skillet. Simmer for 10 minutes, then top with half of the vegan cheese and bake in the oven at 375°F for 10 minutes.
4. For the Mexican Pasta: Add pasta, bell peppers, and the remaining diced tomatoes to the skillet. Pour in water to cover the pasta, bring to a boil, then simmer until the pasta is cooked, about 15 minutes. Stir in the remaining vegan cheese just before serving.
5. For the Cheesy Burger Casserole: Mix the cooked plant-based meat with onions, garlic, and bell peppers in a baking dish. Top with vegan cheese and bake at 375°F for 15 minutes.

Nutritional Facts: (Per serving)

- ❖ Calories: 350
- ❖ Protein: 20g
- ❖ Carbohydrates: 45g
- ❖ Fat: 15g
- ❖ Sodium: 500mg
- ❖ Fiber: 8g

These versatile casseroles provide a delicious way to enjoy a meat-free meal with all the familiar flavors you love. Each recipe is perfect for a cozy night in, offering a comforting and satisfying dining experience.

Chapter 04: Greens in a Bowl

Recipe 31: Vegetables Salads

Enjoy a burst of freshness with this vibrant Vegetarian Salad Bowl, packed with a colorful array of vegetables like cabbage, tomatoes, lettuce, onions, and carrots. This wholesome meal is complemented by two crispy toasts, making it a perfect, light, and nutritious choice for any time of day.

Servings: 4

Prepping Time: 15 minutes

Cook Time: 0 minutes

Difficulty: Easy

Ingredients:

- ✓ 2 cups shredded lettuce
- ✓ 1 cup shredded cabbage
- ✓ 2 tomatoes, chopped
- ✓ 1 onion, thinly sliced
- ✓ 2 carrots, grated
- ✓ 1 cucumber, sliced
- ✓ 1 red bell pepper, sliced
- ✓ 4 slices whole grain bread
- ✓ 2 tablespoons olive oil
- ✓ 1 tablespoon vinegar
- ✓ Salt and pepper to taste
- ✓ Fresh herbs (like parsley or basil), chopped for garnish

Step-by-Step Preparation:

1. In a large bowl, combine lettuce, cabbage, tomatoes, onion, carrots, cucumber, and red bell pepper.
2. In a small bowl, whisk together olive oil, vinegar, salt, and pepper to create a dressing.
3. Pour the dressing over the salad and toss gently to coat all the vegetables evenly.
4. Toast the bread slices until golden and crispy.
5. Serve the salad immediately, garnished with fresh herbs and accompanied by the toast on the side.

Nutritional Facts: (Per serving)

- ❖ Calories: 180
- ❖ Protein: 4g
- ❖ Carbohydrates: 27g
- ❖ Fat: 7g
- ❖ Sodium: 200mg
- ❖ Fiber: 5g

This salad bowl is not just a meal but a colorful canvas of nutrition and flavor, ideal for those seeking a healthy and refreshing dining option. It's a delightful way to enjoy a variety of vegetables in one go, leaving you feeling satisfied and energized.

Recipe 32: Homemade Vegetable Baked Salad

Savor the roasted goodness of a Homemade Vegetable Baked Salad, where yellow zucchini, red peppers, and tomatoes come together under a medley of herbs to create a delicious and visually stunning dish. Topped with fresh coriander, this warm salad is a delightful twist on traditional greens, making it a perfect side or main dish.

Servings: 4

Prepping Time: 15 minutes

Cook Time: 25 minutes

Difficulty: Easy

Ingredients:

- ✓ 1 yellow zucchini, sliced
- ✓ 2 red peppers, sliced
- ✓ 3 tomatoes, quartered
- ✓ 1/4 cup fresh coriander, chopped
- ✓ 2 tablespoons olive oil
- ✓ 1 teaspoon salt
- ✓ 1/2 teaspoon black pepper
- ✓ 1 teaspoon dried oregano

Step-by-Step Preparation:

1. Preheat your oven to 375°F (190°C).
2. In a large bowl, combine the sliced zucchini, red peppers, and quartered tomatoes.
3. Drizzle with olive oil, then season with salt, pepper, and dried oregano. Toss everything together to ensure the vegetables are evenly coated.
4. Spread the vegetables on a baking sheet in a single layer.
5. Bake in the preheated oven for 25 minutes, or until the vegetables are tender and slightly caramelized.
6. Remove from the oven and sprinkle with fresh coriander before serving.

Nutritional Facts: (Per serving)

- ❖ Calories: 90
- ❖ Protein: 2g
- ❖ Carbohydrates: 10g
- ❖ Fat: 5g
- ❖ Sodium: 590mg
- ❖ Fiber: 3g

This Homemade Vegetable Baked Salad is a feast for the senses, offering a satisfying crunch and burst of flavors that elevate your mealtime. It's an ideal recipe for those looking to add a healthy and colorful touch to their dining table.

Recipe 33: Baked Vegetable Mix Salad

Indulge in the heartwarming flavors of a Baked Vegetable Mix Salad, where sliced broccoli, potato, and sweet potato meld together under a blanket of melted cheese and aromatic herbs. This comforting dish brings together the best of wholesome ingredients and savory seasonings for a delightful vegetarian experience.

Servings: 4

Prepping Time: 15 minutes

Cook Time: 35 minutes

Difficulty: Easy

Ingredients:

- ✓ 1 large potato, thinly sliced
- ✓ 1 large sweet potato, thinly sliced
- ✓ 2 cups broccoli florets
- ✓ 1 cup grated cheese (choose a type that melts well, like cheddar or mozzarella)
- ✓ 2 tablespoons olive oil
- ✓ 1 teaspoon dried rosemary
- ✓ 1 teaspoon dried thyme
- ✓ Salt and pepper to taste

Step-by-Step Preparation:

1. Preheat your oven to 400°F (200°C).
2. In a large mixing bowl, combine the sliced potatoes, sweet potatoes, and broccoli florets.
3. Drizzle with olive oil, and sprinkle with rosemary, thyme, salt, and pepper. Toss well to ensure all the vegetables are evenly coated.
4. Arrange the vegetables in a single layer on a baking sheet.
5. Sprinkle the grated cheese evenly over the top of the vegetables.
6. Bake in the preheated oven for about 35 minutes, or until the vegetables are tender and the cheese is bubbly and golden.
7. Serve hot, directly from the oven.

Nutritional Facts: (Per serving)

- ❖ Calories: 300
- ❖ Protein: 10g
- ❖ Carbohydrates: 34g
- ❖ Fat: 15g
- ❖ Sodium: 220mg
- ❖ Fiber: 5g

This Baked Vegetable Mix Salad is a perfect blend of simplicity and flavor, ideal for a cozy evening meal or as a hearty side dish. Its warm, cheesy goodness makes it a crowd-pleaser at any table.

Recipe 34: Vegetable Chicken Pasta Salad

Experience the vibrant flavors of the Mediterranean with this One Pot Mediterranean Vegetable Pasta Salad, a colorful and healthy dish that combines pasta with a bounty of fresh vegetables. This vegetarian salad is perfect for any meal, providing a satisfying blend of textures and tastes that embody the freshness of the region.

Servings: 4

Prepping Time: 10 minutes

Cook Time: 15 minutes

Difficulty: Easy

Ingredients:

- ✓ 8 oz penne pasta
- ✓ 1 zucchini, sliced
- ✓ 1 red bell pepper, chopped
- ✓ 1 cup cherry tomatoes, halved
- ✓ 1/2 cup Kalamata olives, pitted and halved
- ✓ 1/4 cup red onion, thinly sliced
- ✓ 1/4 cup feta cheese, crumbled
- ✓ 1/4 cup extra virgin olive oil
- ✓ 2 tablespoons red wine vinegar
- ✓ 1 garlic clove, minced
- ✓ 1 teaspoon dried oregano
- ✓ Salt and pepper to taste
- ✓ Fresh basil leaves, for garnish

Step-by-Step Preparation:

1. Cook the penne pasta in a large pot of boiling salted water according to package instructions until al dente; drain and rinse under cold water to cool.
2. In a large bowl, combine the cooked pasta with zucchini, red bell pepper, cherry tomatoes, olives, and red onion.
3. In a small bowl, whisk together the olive oil, red wine vinegar, minced garlic, oregano, salt, and pepper to create the dressing.
4. Pour the dressing over the pasta and vegetables and toss gently to coat evenly.
5. Sprinkle crumbled feta cheese over the top and garnish with fresh basil leaves.
6. Serve chilled or at room temperature.

Nutritional Facts: (Per serving)

- ❖ Calories: 350
- ❖ Protein: 9g
- ❖ Carbohydrates: 44g
- ❖ Fat: 17g
- ❖ Sodium: 320mg
- ❖ Fiber: 4g

This One Pot Mediterranean Vegetable Pasta Salad is not just a meal; it's a vibrant celebration of summer flavors that brings a touch of the Mediterranean to your table. It's perfect for a refreshing lunch or a light dinner, especially on warm days.

Recipe 35: Roasted and Marinated Vegetables Salad

Celebrate the rich flavors of the Mediterranean with a Roasted and Marinated Vegetable Salad, featuring a delightful combination of capers and olives. This dish highlights the robust essence of roasted vegetables, enhanced by the tangy zest of marination, making it an exquisite choice for a healthful and tantalizing meal.

Servings: 4

Prepping Time: 15 minutes

Cook Time: 25 minutes

Difficulty: Easy

Ingredients:

- ✓ 1 red bell pepper, sliced
- ✓ 1 yellow bell pepper, sliced
- ✓ 1 zucchini, sliced
- ✓ 1 eggplant, sliced
- ✓ 1 red onion, sliced
- ✓ 1/4 cup olives, pitted and halved
- ✓ 2 tablespoons capers, rinsed
- ✓ 1/4 cup olive oil
- ✓ 2 tablespoons balsamic vinegar
- ✓ 1 teaspoon dried oregano
- ✓ Salt and pepper to taste
- ✓ Fresh parsley, chopped for garnish

Step-by-Step Preparation:

1. Preheat your oven to 425°F (220°C).
2. Arrange the sliced bell peppers, zucchini, eggplant, and onion on a baking sheet. Drizzle with half of the olive oil and season with salt and pepper.
3. Roast the vegetables in the preheated oven for about 25 minutes or until tender and lightly charred.
4. Remove from the oven and let cool slightly.
5. In a large bowl, combine the roasted vegetables with olives and capers.
6. Whisk together the remaining olive oil, balsamic vinegar, oregano, salt, and pepper to create the dressing.
7. Pour the dressing over the vegetables and toss to coat evenly.
8. Garnish with chopped parsley before serving.

Nutritional Facts: (Per serving)

- ❖ Calories: 200
- ❖ Protein: 2g
- ❖ Carbohydrates: 15g
- ❖ Fat: 15g
- ❖ Sodium: 200mg
- ❖ Fiber: 5g

This Roasted and Marinated Vegetable Salad with Capers and Olives is not just a dish but a vibrant journey through texture and taste. It's perfect for those who appreciate a hearty, flavor-packed salad that can serve as both a main course and a sophisticated side.

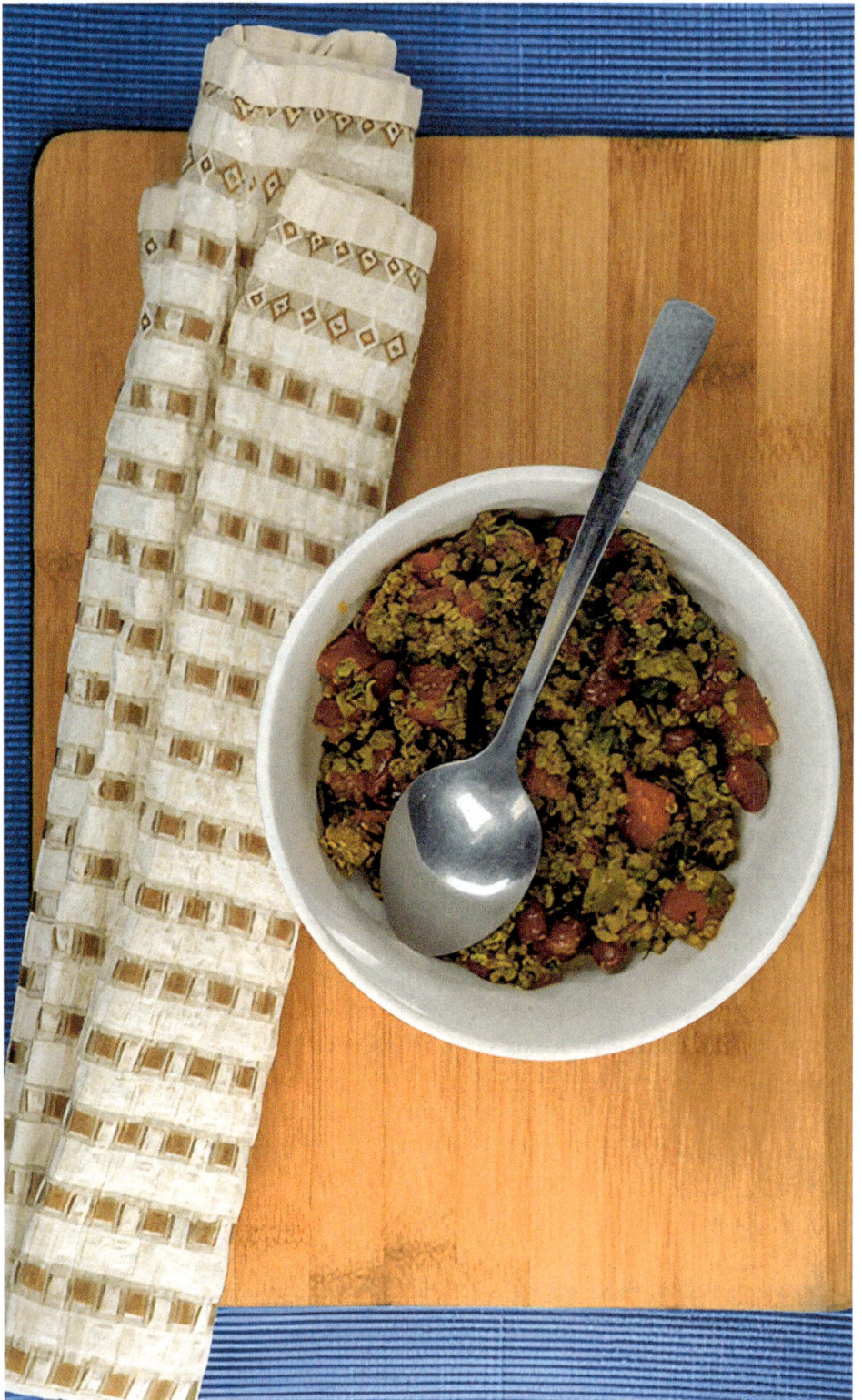

Recipe 36: Healthy Quinoa Salad

Indulge in the delightful flavors of a Delicious and Healthy Quinoa Salad, a perfect blend of fluffy quinoa and crisp vegetables dressed in a tangy vinaigrette. This light yet satisfying dish is ideal for health-conscious diners looking for a nutritious meal that doesn't skimp on taste.

Servings: 4

Cook Time: 15 minutes

Prepping Time: 10 minutes

Difficulty: Easy

Ingredients:

- ✓ 1 cup quinoa
- ✓ 2 cups water
- ✓ 1 cucumber, diced
- ✓ 1 red bell pepper, diced
- ✓ 1/2 red onion, finely chopped
- ✓ 1/4 cup fresh parsley, chopped
- ✓ 1/4 cup olive oil
- ✓ Juice of 1 lemon
- ✓ 1 clove garlic, minced
- ✓ Salt and pepper to taste
- ✓ 1/4 cup feta cheese, crumbled (optional)

Step-by-Step Preparation:

1. Rinse the quinoa under cold water until the water runs clear.
2. In a medium saucepan, combine quinoa and water. Bring to a boil, then reduce heat to low, cover, and simmer for 15 minutes or until the water is absorbed and the quinoa is tender.
3. Fluff the quinoa with a fork and let it cool to room temperature.
4. In a large bowl, mix the cooled quinoa, cucumber, bell pepper, red onion, and parsley.
5. In a small bowl, whisk together olive oil, lemon juice, minced garlic, salt, and pepper to create the dressing.
6. Pour the dressing over the salad and toss to combine thoroughly.
7. Sprinkle with crumbled feta cheese, if using, before serving.

Nutritional Facts: (Per serving)

- ❖ Calories: 290
- ❖ Protein: 8g
- ❖ Carbohydrates: 33g
- ❖ Fat: 15g
- ❖ Sodium: 100mg
- ❖ Fiber: 5g

This Delicious and Healthy Quinoa Salad is the epitome of eating well and feeling great. Its fresh ingredients and zesty flavors make it an ideal choice for a quick lunch or a side dish at dinner, providing both nourishment and pleasure.

Recipe 37: Turkish Food Bulgur Salad - Kisir

Discover the vibrant flavors of Kisir, a traditional Turkish bulgur salad that's as nutritious as it is delicious. This vegetarian dish is a staple in Turkish cuisine, known for its bold spices, fresh herbs, and tangy dressing. Kisir is perfect for a light lunch or a festive side dish, bringing a burst of Mediterranean flair to any table.

Servings: 4

Prepping Time: 15 minutes

Cook Time: 5 minutes

Difficulty: Easy

Ingredients:

- 1 cup fine bulgur
- 1 cup boiling water
- 1 small cucumber, diced
- 2 green onions, chopped
- 1/2 cup fresh parsley, finely chopped
- 1/4 cup fresh mint, finely chopped
- 2 tablespoons tomato paste
- 1/4 cup olive oil
- Juice of 1 lemon
- 1 teaspoon paprika
- Salt and pepper to taste
- 1 teaspoon ground cumin

Step-by-Step Preparation:

1. Place the bulgur in a large bowl and cover with boiling water. Let stand for about 10 minutes until the water is absorbed and the bulgur is tender. Fluff with a fork.

2. Stir in the tomato paste, olive oil, lemon juice, paprika, cumin, salt, and pepper, mixing until the bulgur is well coated.

3. Add the cucumber, green onions, parsley, and mint to the bulgur mixture and toss to combine.

4. Adjust seasoning to taste and let the salad sit for at least 30 minutes before serving to allow the flavors to meld.

Nutritional Facts: (Per serving)

- Calories: 280
- Protein: 6g
- Carbohydrates: 40g
- Fat: 12g
- Sodium: 200mg
- Fiber: 9g

Kisir is not just a meal; it's a colorful celebration of texture and taste that showcases the best of Turkish cuisine. Enjoy this bulgur salad as a standalone dish or pair it with other Mediterranean favorites for a truly festive meal.

Recipe 38: Turkish Green Olives Salad

Embark on a culinary journey with this Turkish Green Olives Salad, a vibrant medley of crisp cucumbers, juicy tomatoes, rich walnuts, and zesty parsley, all brought together by the distinct flavor of green olives. This dish is a celebration of fresh and bold Mediterranean ingredients, perfect for a refreshing side or a light main course.

Servings: 4

Cook Time: 0 minutes

Prepping Time: 10 minutes

Difficulty: Easy

Ingredients:

- ✓ 1 cup green olives, pitted and sliced
- ✓ 1/2 cup walnuts, roughly chopped
- ✓ 2 tomatoes, diced
- ✓ 1 cucumber, diced
- ✓ 1/2 cup fresh parsley, chopped
- ✓ 1/4 cup olive oil
- ✓ Juice of 1 lemon
- ✓ 1 clove garlic, minced
- ✓ Salt and pepper to taste

Step-by-Step Preparation:

1. In a large bowl, combine the sliced green olives, chopped walnuts, diced tomatoes, and diced cucumber.
2. Add the chopped parsley to the bowl.
3. In a small bowl, whisk together the olive oil, lemon juice, minced garlic, salt, and pepper to create a dressing.
4. Pour the dressing over the salad ingredients and toss gently to coat everything evenly.
5. Let the salad sit for about 5 minutes to allow the flavors to meld before serving.

Nutritional Facts: (Per serving)

- ❖ Calories: 220
- ❖ Protein: 3g
- ❖ Carbohydrates: 8g
- ❖ Fat: 20g
- ❖ Sodium: 400mg
- ❖ Fiber: 3g

This Turkish Green Olives Salad with Walnuts offers a refreshing twist to your salad routine, combining the crunch of walnuts with the tang of olives in a way that's sure to delight your taste buds. It's perfect for those seeking a nutritious, flavor-packed meal that embodies the essence of Turkish flavors.

Recipe 39: Roasted, Grilled Bell Peppers Salad

Immerse yourself in the smoky richness of Roasted Grilled Bell Peppers, dressed elegantly with fresh herbs and a drizzle of olive oil. This simple yet exquisite dish captures the essence of Mediterranean cuisine, featuring charred bell peppers that are as visually stunning as they are delicious. It's a perfect accompaniment to any meal or a standout on its own.

Servings: 4

Prepping Time: 10 minutes

Cook Time: 15 minutes

Difficulty: Easy

Ingredients:

- ✓ 4 bell peppers (red, yellow, and green), halved and seeded
- ✓ 2 tablespoons olive oil

- ✓ 1 tablespoon fresh basil, chopped
- ✓ 1 tablespoon fresh parsley, chopped
- ✓ Salt and pepper to taste

Step-by-Step Preparation:

1. Preheat your grill to medium-high heat.
2. Brush the bell peppers with olive oil on both sides and season with salt and pepper.
3. Place the bell peppers on the grill, skin side down, and cook for about 7-8 minutes or until the skins are charred and blistered.
4. Turn the peppers over and grill for another 7 minutes until the flesh is soft and slightly charred.
5. Remove from the grill and let cool slightly. Once cool enough to handle, peel off the charred skins.
6. Slice the grilled peppers and arrange them on a serving dish.
7. Sprinkle with chopped basil and parsley, and drizzle with a bit more olive oil before serving.

Nutritional Facts: (Per serving)

- ❖ Calories: 90
- ❖ Protein: 1g
- ❖ Carbohydrates: 6g

- ❖ Fat: 7g
- ❖ Sodium: 5mg
- ❖ Fiber: 2g

This Roasted Grilled Bell Peppers dish is not just a treat for the palate but also a feast for the eyes, with its vibrant colors and rustic charm. It's a delightful way to enjoy the natural sweetness of bell peppers, enhanced by the freshness of herbs and the richness of olive oil.

Recipe 40: Tomatoes With Arugula Pesto Salad

Experience the zesty burst of flavors in the Tomatoes with Arugula Pesto Salad, where juicy tomatoes are paired with a vibrant arugula pesto, mushrooms, olives, and capers. This salad brings together fresh, tangy ingredients, creating a dish that's as delightful to the palate as it is to the eyes, perfect for a light meal or a side dish.

Servings: 4

Prepping Time: 15 minutes

Cook Time: 0 minutes

Difficulty: Easy

Ingredients:

- ✓ 4 large ripe tomatoes, sliced
- ✓ 1 cup fresh arugula
- ✓ 1/2 cup fresh basil leaves
- ✓ 1/4 cup grated Parmesan cheese
- ✓ 1/4 cup pine nuts
- ✓ 2 cloves garlic
- ✓ 1/2 cup olive oil
- ✓ 1/2 cup sliced mushrooms
- ✓ 1/4 cup black olives, sliced
- ✓ 2 tablespoons capers
- ✓ Salt and pepper to taste

Step-by-Step Preparation:

1. In a food processor, blend arugula, basil, Parmesan cheese, pine nuts, and garlic into a coarse paste.
2. Slowly pour in the olive oil while the processor is running, until the pesto reaches your desired consistency. Season with salt and pepper.
3. Arrange the sliced tomatoes on a serving platter.
4. Top the tomatoes with sliced mushrooms, olives, and capers.
5. Drizzle the arugula pesto over the salad.
6. Serve immediately, allowing the flavors to meld together briefly before enjoying.

Nutritional Facts: (Per serving)

- ❖ Calories: 320
- ❖ Protein: 6g
- ❖ Carbohydrates: 8g
- ❖ Fat: 30g
- ❖ Sodium: 380mg
- ❖ Fiber: 3g

This Tomatoes with Arugula Pesto Salad is a celebration of Mediterranean flavors, combining the freshness of garden produce with the boldness of pesto for a uniquely satisfying culinary experience. Perfect for those who enjoy a dish that's as healthy as it is flavorful.

Chapter 05: Cozy Sips

Recipe 41: Homemade Minestrone Soup

Delve into the hearty and wholesome world of traditional Italian cuisine with this homemade Minestrone Soup. A quintessential one-pot dish, it features a robust medley of tomatoes, carrots, onions, savoy cabbage, cannellini beans, celery, and potatoes, each contributing to a deeply flavorful and nourishing meal perfect for any day.

Servings: 6

Prepping Time: 20 minutes

Cook Time: 45 minutes

Difficulty: Easy

Ingredients:

- 2 tablespoons olive oil
- 1 large onion, chopped
- 2 carrots, peeled and diced
- 2 stalks celery, diced
- 3 potatoes, peeled and cubed
- 1/2 head savoy cabbage, chopped
- 1 can (15 oz) cannellini beans, drained and rinsed
- 1 can (14.5 oz) diced tomatoes

- 6 cups vegetable broth
- 2 cloves garlic, minced
- 1 teaspoon dried basil
- 1 teaspoon dried oregano
- Salt and pepper to taste
- Fresh parsley, chopped for garnish
- Grated Parmesan cheese, for serving (optional)

Step-by-Step Preparation:

1. Heat olive oil in a large pot over medium heat. Add onions, carrots, and celery, and sauté until the onions are translucent, about 5 minutes.
2. Add garlic and continue to cook for another minute until fragrant.
3. Stir in the potatoes, cabbage, cannellini beans, and diced tomatoes. Pour in the vegetable broth.
4. Season with dried basil, oregano, salt, and pepper. Bring to a boil, then reduce heat and let simmer for about 30 minutes, or until the vegetables are tender.
5. Adjust seasoning to taste, and add more broth if the soup is too thick.
6. Serve hot, garnished with chopped parsley and a sprinkle of grated Parmesan cheese if desired.

Nutritional Facts: (Per serving)

- Calories: 210
- Protein: 7g
- Carbohydrates: 38g

- Fat: 4g
- Sodium: 700mg
- Fiber: 8g

This Minestrone Soup offers a comforting taste of Italy in every spoonful, celebrating the simplicity and richness of flavors that define Italian home cooking.

Recipe 42: Egusi Is a Traditional One-Pot Soup

Dive into the rich and savory world of Egusi Soup, a traditional one-pot dish that's a staple in West African cuisine. This vegetarian version combines the nutty flavor of ground melon seeds with vibrant peppers, leafy greens, and hearty potatoes, creating a comforting and nutritious meal that's full of texture and taste.

Servings: 4

Prepping Time: 20 minutes

Cook Time: 30 minutes

Difficulty: Medium

Ingredients:

- ✓ 1 cup ground egusi (melon seeds)
- ✓ 2 large potatoes, peeled and cubed
- ✓ 1 bell pepper, blended
- ✓ 2 cups spinach, washed and chopped
- ✓ 1 onion, chopped
- ✓ 2 cloves garlic, minced
- ✓ 4 cups vegetable broth
- ✓ 2 tablespoons palm oil (or substitute with vegetable oil)
- ✓ 1 teaspoon cayenne pepper
- ✓ Salt to taste

Step-by-Step Preparation:

1. Heat the palm oil in a large pot over medium heat. Add onions and garlic, sautéing until soft and translucent.
2. Stir in the blended bell pepper and cook for about 5 minutes, allowing the flavors to meld.
3. Add the ground egusi seeds to the pot and stir continuously for another 5 minutes.
4. Pour in the vegetable broth, bring the mixture to a boil, then reduce the heat to a simmer.
5. Add the cubed potatoes to the pot and let simmer for about 15 minutes, or until the potatoes are tender.
6. Stir in the chopped spinach and season with cayenne pepper and salt. Cook for an additional 5 minutes.
7. Adjust seasoning to taste, and add more broth if the soup is too thick.

Nutritional Facts: (Per serving)

- ❖ Calories: 256
- ❖ Protein: 8g
- ❖ Carbohydrates: 25g
- ❖ Fat: 14g
- ❖ Sodium: 300mg
- ❖ Fiber: 5g

This Egusi Soup is a delightful exploration of African culinary traditions, bringing a unique blend of flavors and textures to your dining table. It's perfect for anyone looking to expand their culinary horizons with a hearty, wholesome soup that satisfies every spoonful.

Recipe 43: Vegan Vegetable Soup

Warm up with a bowl of fresh homemade Vegan Vegetable Soup, brimming with nutritious ingredients like kale, chickpeas, carrots, celery, onions, and potatoes. This hearty one-pot soup is a perfect blend of comfort and health, offering a delicious way to enjoy a variety of vegetables in one satisfying meal.

Servings: 4

Cook Time: 30 minutes

Prepping Time: 15 minutes

Difficulty: Easy

Ingredients:

- ✓ 1 cup chickpeas, cooked or canned
- ✓ 2 large carrots, diced
- ✓ 2 celery stalks, diced
- ✓ 1 large onion, chopped
- ✓ 2 potatoes, cubed
- ✓ 2 cups kale, chopped
- ✓ 1 tablespoon olive oil
- ✓ 6 cups vegetable broth
- ✓ 1 teaspoon salt
- ✓ 1/2 teaspoon black pepper
- ✓ 1 teaspoon dried thyme

Step-by-Step Preparation:

1. Heat olive oil in a large pot over medium heat. Add onions, carrots, and celery, sautéing until the onions are translucent and fragrant.
2. Add potatoes and cooked chickpeas to the pot, stirring to combine.
3. Pour in the vegetable broth and bring the mixture to a boil.
4. Reduce heat to a simmer and add the kale, salt, pepper, and thyme.
5. Let the soup simmer for about 20 minutes or until the vegetables are tender.
6. Adjust seasoning to taste and serve hot.

Nutritional Facts: (Per serving)

- ❖ Calories: 230
- ❖ Protein: 8g
- ❖ Carbohydrates: 42g
- ❖ Fat: 4g
- ❖ Sodium: 800mg
- ❖ Fiber: 9g

This Vegan Vegetable Soup is a nourishing delight, perfect for cold days or anytime you need a comforting meal that's packed with flavor and nutrients. It's a simple, easy-to-make dish that showcases the best of what plant-based eating has to offer.

Recipe 44: One Pot Vegetable Soup

Embrace the flavors of a garden in your bowl with this One Pot Vegetable Soup, featuring a comforting blend of cauliflower, courgette (zucchini), tomatoes, carrots, and fennel. This light yet hearty soup is perfect for those seeking a delicious way to enjoy a variety of vegetables, all simmered together to create a flavorful and nourishing meal.

Servings: 4

Prepping Time: 15 minutes

Cook Time: 30 minutes

Difficulty: Easy

Ingredients:

- ✓ 1 cauliflower head, chopped
- ✓ 1 courgette (zucchini), sliced
- ✓ 3 tomatoes, chopped
- ✓ 2 carrots, diced
- ✓ 1 fennel bulb, chopped
- ✓ 1 onion, diced
- ✓ 2 cloves garlic, minced
- ✓ 6 cups vegetable broth
- ✓ 2 tablespoons olive oil
- ✓ Salt and pepper to taste
- ✓ 1 teaspoon dried thyme

Step-by-Step Preparation:

1. Heat olive oil in a large pot over medium heat. Add the onion and garlic, and sauté until the onion becomes translucent.

2. Add the carrots, fennel, cauliflower, and courgette to the pot, stirring to mix with the onions and garlic.

3. Stir in the chopped tomatoes and dried thyme, cooking for a few minutes until the tomatoes start to break down.

4. Pour in the vegetable broth and bring the mixture to a boil. Reduce heat to a simmer and cover the pot.

5. Let the soup cook for about 25 minutes, or until all vegetables are tender.

6. Season with salt and pepper to taste. Serve hot.

Nutritional Facts: (Per serving)

- ❖ Calories: 180
- ❖ Protein: 5g
- ❖ Carbohydrates: 25g
- ❖ Fat: 7g
- ❖ Sodium: 480mg
- ❖ Fiber: 6g

This One Pot Vegetable Soup is a testament to how simple ingredients can be transformed into a deeply satisfying dish. It's perfect for a cozy night in or a nutritious lunch, offering a wholesome and tasty way to warm up any day.

Recipe 45: Onion Soup With Dried Bread

Delve into the comforting embrace of this classic Onion Soup, enriched with the robust flavors of caramelized onions, topped with dried bread and melted cheddar cheese. This vegetarian version offers a hearty, warming dish that is perfect for chilly evenings, combining simple ingredients that pack a flavorful punch.

Servings: 4

Cook Time: 45 minutes

Prepping Time: 15 minutes

Difficulty: Medium

Ingredients:

- 4 large onions, thinly sliced
- 4 slices of dried bread
- 1 cup shredded cheddar cheese
- 4 cups vegetable broth
- 2 tablespoons butter
- 1 teaspoon sugar
- 1 teaspoon balsamic vinegar
- 1 bay leaf
- Salt and pepper to taste
- Fresh thyme, for garnish

Step-by-Step Preparation:

1. In a large pot, melt the butter over medium heat. Add the onions and sugar, cooking slowly until the onions are deeply caramelized, about 30 minutes, stirring occasionally to prevent burning.

2. Add balsamic vinegar and a bay leaf, and cook for another 5 minutes.

3. Pour in the vegetable broth and bring the mixture to a simmer. Season with salt and pepper.

4. Preheat the broiler.

5. Place the dried bread slices in a single layer on a baking sheet and sprinkle evenly with shredded cheddar cheese. Broil until the cheese is bubbly and golden brown.

6. To serve, ladle the hot soup into bowls. Top each bowl with a cheese-topped bread slice. Garnish with fresh thyme.

Nutritional Facts: (Per serving)

- Calories: 290
- Protein: 12g
- Carbohydrates: 34g
- Fat: 12g
- Sodium: 960mg
- Fiber: 4g

This Onion Soup with Dried Bread and Cheddar Cheese serves as a delightful reminder of the power of simple, well-cooked ingredients to transform into a deeply satisfying meal. It's perfect for anyone seeking comfort in a bowl, especially on those colder days.

Recipe 46: Forest Mushroom Soup

Step into the earthy, wild flavors of the forest with this Forest Mushroom Soup. A blend of various mushrooms gathered from the woods, this soup encapsulates a rich and aromatic experience that is both comforting and luxurious. Perfect for those who appreciate the deep, umami-packed flavors of forest-grown fungi.

Servings: 4

Prepping Time: 20 minutes

Cook Time: 30 minutes

Difficulty: Easy

Ingredients:

- ✓ 3 cups mixed wild mushrooms, cleaned and chopped (such as morels, chanterelles, and porcini)
- ✓ 1 onion, finely chopped
- ✓ 2 cloves garlic, minced
- ✓ 4 cups vegetable broth
- ✓ 1 cup heavy cream
- ✓ 2 tablespoons butter
- ✓ 1 teaspoon dried thyme
- ✓ Salt and pepper to taste
- ✓ Fresh parsley, chopped for garnish
- ✓ 1 tablespoon olive oil

Step-by-Step Preparation:

1. In a large pot, heat the butter and olive oil over medium heat. Add the onion and garlic, sautéing until translucent and fragrant.

2. Add the chopped mushrooms and thyme, cooking until the mushrooms are golden and have released their juices, about 10 minutes.

3. Pour in the vegetable broth and bring to a boil. Reduce heat and simmer for 20 minutes to melt the flavors.

4. Stir in the heavy cream, and continue to simmer for another 5 minutes. Season with salt and pepper to taste.

5. Serve hot, garnished with fresh parsley.

Nutritional Facts: (Per serving)

- ❖ Calories: 310
- ❖ Protein: 5g
- ❖ Carbohydrates: 12g
- ❖ Fat: 28g
- ❖ Sodium: 950mg
- ❖ Fiber: 2g

This Forest Mushroom Soup is a delightful retreat into nature's pantry, offering a taste of the wild in every spoonful. It's perfect for warming up on a chilly day or impressing guests with its sophisticated flavor profile.

Recipe 47: Vegan Penne Vegetable Soup

Immerse yourself in the heartiness of Vegan Penne Vegetable Soup, a vibrant dish brimming with colorful vegetables and tender penne pasta. This soup is a delightful celebration of flavors and textures, providing a comforting and satisfying meal that's both nutritious and easy to prepare, making it perfect for any day of the week.

Servings: 4

Prepping Time: 15 minutes

Cook Time: 20 minutes

Difficulty: Easy

Ingredients:

- ✓ 1 cup penne pasta, uncooked
- ✓ 1 carrot, diced
- ✓ 1 zucchini, diced
- ✓ 1 red bell pepper, diced
- ✓ 1 onion, chopped
- ✓ 2 cloves garlic, minced
- ✓ 4 cups vegetable broth
- ✓ 1 can (14.5 oz) diced tomatoes
- ✓ 1 teaspoon dried basil
- ✓ 1 teaspoon dried oregano
- ✓ 2 tablespoons olive oil
- ✓ Salt and pepper to taste
- ✓ Fresh basil, for garnish

Step-by-Step Preparation:

1. Heat olive oil in a large pot over medium heat. Add onion and garlic, and sauté until translucent.
2. Add carrots, zucchini, and red bell pepper, sautéing for a few minutes until slightly softened.
3. Pour in the vegetable broth and diced tomatoes. Stir in dried basil and oregano. Bring to a boil.
4. Add the penne pasta to the boiling soup and cook according to the package instructions until al dente.
5. Season with salt and pepper. Adjust the seasoning if necessary.
6. Serve hot, garnished with fresh basil leaves.

Nutritional Facts: (Per serving)

- ❖ Calories: 280
- ❖ Protein: 8g
- ❖ Carbohydrates: 46g
- ❖ Fat: 7g
- ❖ Sodium: 800mg
- ❖ Fiber: 6g

This Vegan Penne Vegetable Soup is a wonderful way to enjoy a fulfilling meal that is both flavorful and hearty. It combines the robust tastes of fresh vegetables with the comfort of pasta in a single pot, ensuring a quick, delicious, and comforting meal suitable for any occasion.

Recipe 48: Soup With Cabbage and Carrots

Enjoy the comforting flavors of this Vegetable Soup with Cabbage and Carrot, a simple yet delicious blend of nutritious vegetables. This one-pot soup is a fantastic way to warm up on a chilly day, offering a hearty and healthy meal that's both filling and easy to prepare.

Servings: 4

Cook Time: 30 minutes

Prepping Time: 10 minutes

Difficulty: Easy

Ingredients:

- ✓ 1/2 head cabbage, chopped
- ✓ 2 carrots, peeled and diced
- ✓ 1 onion, chopped
- ✓ 2 cloves garlic, minced
- ✓ 4 cups vegetable broth
- ✓ 1 teaspoon thyme
- ✓ 1 tablespoon olive oil
- ✓ Salt and pepper to taste
- ✓ Fresh parsley, chopped for garnish

Step-by-Step Preparation:

1. Heat olive oil in a large pot over medium heat. Add onions and garlic, sautéing until the onions are translucent.

2. Add the carrots and cabbage to the pot, stirring for a few minutes until they start to soften.

3. Pour in the vegetable broth and add thyme. Bring the mixture to a boil, then reduce heat to a simmer.

4. Simmer for about 20 minutes, or until all vegetables are tender.

5. Season with salt and pepper to taste.

6. Serve hot, garnished with fresh parsley.

Nutritional Facts: (Per serving)

- ❖ Calories: 90
- ❖ Protein: 2g
- ❖ Carbohydrates: 15g
- ❖ Fat: 3g
- ❖ Sodium: 950mg
- ❖ Fiber: 4g

This Vegetable Soup with Cabbage and Carrot is perfect for those seeking a light yet satisfying meal. It's a wholesome dish that not only nourishes the body but also comforts the soul with its rich flavors and aromatic warmth.

Recipe 49: Cauliflower Cream Soup

Dive into the creamy delight of this vegetarian Cauliflower Cream Soup, enhanced with the earthy flavors of champignon mushrooms and a touch of celery. This rich, velvety soup blends smooth creaminess with deep umami notes, offering a luxurious and comforting dining experience perfect for any season.

Servings: 4

Prepping Time: 15 minutes

Cook Time: 25 minutes

Difficulty: Easy

Ingredients:

- ✓ 1 head cauliflower, cut into florets
- ✓ 1 cup champignon mushrooms, sliced
- ✓ 1/2 cup celery, chopped
- ✓ 1 onion, chopped
- ✓ 2 cloves garlic, minced
- ✓ 4 cups vegetable broth
- ✓ 1 cup heavy cream
- ✓ 2 tablespoons olive oil
- ✓ Salt and pepper to taste
- ✓ Fresh chives, chopped for garnish

Step-by-Step Preparation:

1. Heat olive oil in a large pot over medium heat. Add onion and garlic, sauté until soft and translucent.
2. Add the cauliflower, mushrooms, and celery to the pot, stirring for a few minutes until the vegetables begin to soften.
3. Pour in the vegetable broth and bring to a boil. Reduce heat and simmer for 20 minutes, or until all vegetables are tender.
4. Remove from heat. Using an immersion blender, purée the soup until smooth and creamy.
5. Stir in the heavy cream and warm the soup gently. Do not allow it to boil. Season with salt and pepper.
6. Serve hot, garnished with chopped chives.

Nutritional Facts: (Per serving)

- ❖ Calories: 290
- ❖ Protein: 5g
- ❖ Carbohydrates: 18g
- ❖ Fat: 23g
- ❖ Sodium: 450mg
- ❖ Fiber: 4g

This Cauliflower Cream Soup with Champignon Mushrooms and Celery is a testament to the power of simple ingredients, transforming them into a decadent soup that's both nourishing and indulgent. It's the perfect way to enjoy a cozy meal that feels like a hug in a bowl.

Recipe 50: Soup of Cauliflower, Broccoli and Carrots

Savor the delightful simplicity of a vegetable soup that combines the wholesome goodness of cauliflower, broccoli, and carrots. This light yet hearty soup is a testament to the flavors that come from blending fresh, nutritious vegetables, making it a perfect meal for health-conscious individuals looking for comfort and nourishment in one pot.

Servings: 4

Prepping Time: 10 minutes

Cook Time: 20 minutes

Difficulty: Easy

Ingredients:

- ✓ 1 head cauliflower, chopped
- ✓ 1 head of broccoli, chopped
- ✓ 2 carrots, peeled and diced
- ✓ 1 onion, diced
- ✓ 2 cloves garlic, minced
- ✓ 4 cups vegetable broth
- ✓ 2 tablespoons olive oil
- ✓ Salt and pepper to taste
- ✓ Fresh parsley, chopped for garnish

Step-by-Step Preparation:

1. Heat olive oil in a large pot over medium heat. Add onion and garlic, and sauté until onions are translucent.

2. Add the carrots, cauliflower, and broccoli to the pot, stirring for a few minutes to combine the flavors.

3. Pour in the vegetable broth and bring the mixture to a boil. Reduce heat to a simmer and cook for 15 minutes, or until the vegetables are tender.

4. Season with salt and pepper to taste. Optionally, blend the soup for a smoother consistency or leave it as is for a chunky texture.

5. Serve hot, garnished with fresh parsley.

Nutritional Facts: (Per serving)

- ❖ Calories: 150
- ❖ Protein: 5g
- ❖ Carbohydrates: 20g
- ❖ Fat: 7g
- ❖ Sodium: 480mg
- ❖ Fiber: 6g

This Vegetable Soup of Cauliflower, Broccoli, and Carrots is not just a dish; it's a warm, inviting meal that promises comfort with every spoonful. It's ideal for anyone seeking a quick, delicious way to enjoy their vegetables in a soothing, nourishing broth.

Conclusion

Thank you for exploring the **Perfect Vegetarian One Pot Recipes Cookbook**, a collection of recipes designed to make your cooking experience simpler, healthier, and more flavorful. This cookbook was created to inspire you to enjoy the art of vegetarian cooking without the hassle of complicated techniques or piles of dishes to clean.

With **50 carefully crafted recipes** across five diverse chapters, you've discovered how versatile and satisfying one-pot meals can be:

- ✓ **Breakfasts**: Start your day with nourishing dishes like hearty breakfast skillets and one-pot oatmeal delights.

- ✓ **Lunch**: Enjoy quick and wholesome meals that fuel your day with minimal prep time.

- ✓ **Dinners**: Indulge in comforting dishes like pasta bakes, veggie-packed stews, and creative casseroles.

- ✓ **Salads**: Elevate your greens with one-pot creations that are as hearty as they are fresh.

- ✓ **Soup**: Cozy up with rich, flavorful soups that warm your body and soul.

Each recipe has been authentically crafted and rigorously tested to ensure **perfect flavors and consistency**, making every dish a success. The inclusion of **original, colorful photos** for every recipe adds inspiration, guiding you visually to create meals that look as good as they taste.

The **easy-to-follow instructions** ensure that cooks of all skill levels can confidently prepare each dish, while the **standard color-printed paperback** format makes this book both beautiful and functional. Every detail, from the tested flavors to the error-free content, has been designed to provide you with a seamless and enjoyable cooking experience.

Cooking vegetarian meals in one pot is more than just convenient—it's an opportunity to explore bold flavors, simplify your kitchen routine, and enjoy wholesome food every day. This cookbook was created to empower you to bring delicious, plant-based dishes to your table with ease.

Thank you for choosing the **Perfect Vegetarian One Pot Recipes Cookbook**. May these recipes continue to inspire your culinary creativity and bring joy to your meals. Happy cooking!

Printed in Dunstable, United Kingdom